Epiphanies
Through Wisdom Comes Success

BLACK AND WHITE — 2ND EDITION

FOREWORD BY DR. JIM OMPS

KEN 'DR. SMILEY' ROCHON, JR., PhD

Ephiphanies

By Ken 'Dr. Smiley' Rochon, Jr., PhD

Black and White – 2nd Edition

ISBN: 978-1-64810-177-9

PRINTED IN THE UNITED STATES OF AMERICA

PhD Dissertation Program for Entreprenology

"Entreprenology is the study of how (business) knowledge creates abundance" ~ Dr. Ken 'Smiley' Rochon, Jr.

"We but mirror the world. All the tendencies present in the outer world are to be found in the world of our body. If we could change ourselves, the tendencies in the world would also change. As a man changes his own nature, so does the attitude of the world change towards him. This is the divine mystery supreme. A wonderful thing it is and the source of our happiness. We not wait to see what others do." – Mahatma Gandhi

"The Nobelist Art is that of Making Others Happy" - P.T. Barnum

"I will not let anyone walk through my mind with their dirty feet."
~ Mahatma Ghandi

'Have you ever imagined a world with no hypothetical questions?'

THE BOTTOM LINE
~ Author Unknown

THE BOTTOM LINE

FACE IT, nobody owes you a living.

What you achieve, or fail to achieve in your lifetime

Is directly related to what you do or fail to do.

No one chooses his parent or childhood,

But you can choose your own direction.

Everyone has problems and obstacles to overcome,

But that too is relative to each individual.

NOTHING IS CARVED IN STONE!

You can change anything in your life

If you want to badly enough.

Excuses are for losers! Those who take responsibility for their actions

Are the real winners in life.

Winners meet life challenges head on

Knowing there are no guarantees, and give it all they've got

And never think it's too late or too early to begin.

Time plays no favorites

And will pass whether you act or not

Take control of your LIFE

Dare to Dream and take risks.......

Compete!

If you aren't willing to work for your goals

Don't expect others to.

BELIEVE IN YOURSELF!

Acknowledgements & Dedication

For My Son, Kenny (K3). Hope this Wisdom takes you where you want to go.

Thank you, Dad & Mom who enlightened me, with a childhood of acceptance, curiosity, love and wonder.

Nelly who supports me chasing my dreams and imagina- tion one can make a huge difference.

The Happiness & Joy Club: Andrea Adams-Miller, Barry Shore, & Scott Carson

The Legacy Team: Al Granger & Carolyn Sheltraw. The Legacy partners I am honored to have created books with: Gordon Bernhardt, Dr. Latangela Crossfield and Jen Du Plessis.

The HOPE Dealers: Dr. June Davidson, Dr. Janet Smith Warfield & Wm. Paul Young

The Entreprenology Team: Dr. Jim Omps, & Dr. Pauline Crawford Omps for which this book would not have come to the world... so soon.

Friends supporting the possibilities of so many Epiphanies: David Corbin, Ken & Kerri Courtright, Jerry Edwards, Dr. Emily Letran, Joan Magill, Dr. Greg Reid.

Always to my godfather Mark Yessian, my godson, Lucas Richardson, my best men David Richardson, & John Paul Berry.

And all the supporters of connections, and pathways to wisdom: Aaron Murakami, Adam M. Grant, Adam Markel, Al Blackford, Al Granger, Alec Pangia, Alex Charfen, AJ Puedan, Alejandro Brooks, Alex Lowy, Alicia Couri, Allan Karl, Allen Wilterdink, Alyscia Cunningham, Amanda Holmes, Dr. Andrea Adams Miller, Andrea Partee, Andrea Swensen, Angel Ribo, Angel Tuccy, Anik Singal, Anil Gupta, Anniece Acker, Dr. Antoine Chevalier, Aristotle Karas, Avital Miller, Aviv Tene, Baharak Reza, Dr. Barb Hughson, Barbara Palmer, Barry Shore, Baz Porter, Becca Tebon, Ben Gay III, Ben Rudrud, Ben Ward, Bert Oliva, Beth Perl Berman, Bill Voelp, Bob Burg, Brian Basilico, Brian Breen, Brian G. Johnson, Brian Swanson, Calvin Ball, Caren Glasser, Dr. Carl Wilson, Jr., Carol Boyer, Carolyn McGee, Carolyn Owens, Carolyn Sheltraw, Cat Downing, Catherine Pellecchia Perry, Charles Jeff Buck, Charles Byrd, Sir Charles Cary, Chelsea Cushing, Chris Salem, Chef Ciana Kersey, Craig Chasky, Craig Duswalt, Christoff Weihman, Colette Smith, Chris Merriman, Colin Wiebe, Corey Peterson, Cosimo Intermite, Cynthia Murphy, Damon Ehrlich, Dan Chang, Dan Clark, Darius O. 'Doc Renaissance' Gaymon, Darlene Franklin, Dave Farrow, Dave Phillipson, David Corbin, David Hare, David Jackson, David Richardson, Davide Di Giorgio, Dean Pearson, Denise Conde, Dennis Yu, Destiny Magg'ett, Diana Davis, Dolf de Roos, Dorey Jamison, Doug Butschky, Doug Sandler, Drew Berman, Drew Davidsen, Duncan McClintock, Dustin Matthews, Dylan King, Eddie Latimer, Eddie Middlebrooks, Edward Rodriguez, Elsa 'Elsa M' Medhin, Emerson Brantley, Emi Archuleta, Erin Baer, Dr. Fab Mancini, Felipe I Vasquez, Ferlie Almonte, Gary Armstrong, Gayela Bynum, Geetha Krishnan, Genesis Gomez, Gerald Smiley, Gordon Bernhardt, Greg Babcock, Greg Jacobson, Dr. Greg S. Reid, Hannah Kirkpatrick, Harry Lay, Havilande Lodge, Heather Rine, Henry Cho, Insa Ndiaye, Dr. Ivan Misner, Ivy Hutchison, J Shoop, Jack Canfield, Jackson Crisp, James Aquila, Dr. James Dentley, James Evanow, Dr. James Omps, Janelle Harris, Dr. Janet Smith Warfield, Jason Stock, Jay Fiset, Jay Jones, Jeff Hoffman, Jeff Vankooten, Jeffrey Hayzlett, Jen Du Plessis, Jennifer Horspool, Jerry Edwards, Jerry Schwartz, Joe L. Cottrell, Joel Comm, Joey Joyful, Dr. John Gray, John Thompson, Jon Ponder, Jonathan Green, Jordan Edwards, Joseph Terp, Judy Templeton, Julia Hull, Kala Rochelle, Kali O'Campo, Kameren Dawson, Karen Eastman, Kasezga Tembo, Katie Brooks, Keith Leon S, Ken Ashby, Ken Chaletzky, Ken D. Foster, Ken Krell, Ken McArthur, Ken Walls,

Kennedy J. Gilbertson, Kenneth Fontan, Kenneth Lord, Kennon Fort, Kenny Aronoff, Kenny Harper, Kent Emmons, Kent Georgi, Kevin Honeycutt, Dr. Kevin Ross Emery, Kimberly Ross-Hollingsworth, Kurt P. White, Kyle McGregor, Laura Duksta, Laura Poindexter, Lea Tran, Lee Johnson, Leonard Raskin, Dr. Lidie Louis, Lisa Love, Lizette LaForge, Lou Edwards, Loren Michaels Harris, Lowell Sheets, LuAn Mitchell, LuAnn Buechler, Dr. Lydie Louis, Lyman A. Montgomery, Maimah Karmo, Manny Lopez, Mark Goodman, Mark Krekeler, Mark Osborne, Mark Harris, Mark Rober, Matt Attman, Matt Bacak, Dr. Maureen McIntosh-Alberts, Dr. Mel Albin, Michael Neal, Michaela Pratt, Mark Osborne, Melody Garcia, Mery Dominguez, Michael Colyar, Michael Drew, Michael Gerber, Michael Hobson, Michael Schmidlen, Michael Teitelbaum, Michelle Mras, Middleton Evans, Mike Chasman, Mike Corelli, Mike Mellion, Monika Krimendahl, Muhammad Siddique, Nancy Alert, Nancy Ogilvie, Nancy Spencer, Nathan Cassar, Nicholas Kusmich, Nick Valicic, Nico Longoria, Nita Patel, Noelle Peterson, Orly Amor, Oron Harris, Otto Borsich, Ozzy Ramos, Pas Simpson, Patricia Watts, Paul Hoyt, Perry Belcher, Peter Anthony, Peter Strople, Phil Randazzo, Preshona Ambri, Dr. Randi Ward, Ray Leonard Jr., Ray Persinger, Reginald Butler, Renee Piane, Dr. Rich Castello, Rich Parsons, Rick Lewis, Rick Rhodes, RJ Redden, Rob Angel, Robert Ciolino, Robert Clancey, Robert Peterson, Rodney Allgood, Roger Salam, Roland Fraser, Ron Klien, Ron Monk, Roxie Griego, Roz Mansouri, Ryan Treasure, Ryan Walburn, Sally Wurr, Sam Natella, Sarah Coolidge, Sarah Fuentes, Dr. Sarah Renee Langley, Sir Samuel Marx, Scott Carson, Scott Duffy, Sharon Brown, Shaun Callahan, Shaun Runacres, Dr. Stafford Sutton, Stephen Gaffney, Steve Farber, Steve Martin, Dr. Steve Taubman, Steven Wright, Tanya Waltrick, Ted Peterson, Teresa de Grosbois, Terha Watterson, Tien Wong, Tim Ferriss, Tim Kerin, Tim Konig, Tim Mai, Todd Dotson, Todd Westra, Tom Beal, Tony Schumacher, Tula Stamas, Ty Cohen, Umar Hameed, Victor Azar, Travon Taylor, V Helena Yancey, Vince Ealey, Vincent Sharps, Dr. Vinny Leonti, Walter O'Brien, Wasi Mohammad, Wayne R. Connell, Dr. Will Moreland, William Peach, Yakov Smirnoff, Zeev Wexler, and Zina Mashin.

In memory of Frank Shankwitz & Rich Wilens

Foreword

I have always been somewhat amused when I read about or hear somebody claim to know the *Secret to Success*. I don't know if he ever told me what the secret to success is or was, but my father – from my earliest childhood memories – must have known it because he was a highly successful entrepreneur time and again and certainly had the wisdom required for success.

Throughout my life dad inspired me with his words and actions, accompanied by simple logic and amazing determination. He often said, "It's not about doing things right, because that will come when you've done them long enough to see mistakes and correct them." He continued, "No ... it's about *doing the right things*." This wisdom has stayed with me across the many decades of my life.

My father reached his senior years and handed the reigns of his legacy of the International University of Entreprenology (IUE) to me. In 2011 and in my role now as President of IUE, I travelled to a significant conference held in Budapest, Hungary focusing on entrepreneurially oriented micro, small and medium enterprises. Here, as no accident, I met a talented female entrepreneur from England. As we shared magical conversations, I discovered she and I were destined to inspire each other with our dreams, mine to continue the legacy that my father started in 1972, and hers to bring wisdom to the gender dynamic relationships men and women can embrace together to lift business to new levels. It was during these conversations that I had an epiphany regarding the peripheral status that women had in the developing discipline of entreprenology. Now was the time to place this central to business and personal success.

Over the course of the next several months, we recognized our colliding dreams were a life and love journey. She and I married, two entrepreneurs with a dream to transform the education of the world. Now Dr Pauline Crawford, she said yes to my marriage proposal and her PhD. We know it was the wisdom of the universe and synchronicity that led us forward living and working together for the next eight years. Our dream to broaden both the scope and vision of entreprenology becomes clear when we meet and teach many creative, innovative, and interesting women and men in the world today.

One of those people is Kenneth James Rochon Jr. or Dr. *Smiley* to a growing number of his fans and followers. It has been our pleasure to get to know Ken over the past 12+ months and see him achieve his PhD in Entreprenology with IUE, shining the light on his experiences and life credentials. He is a highly creative and innovative individual in his own right, he is also a highly articulate writer and published author, having written, compiled, and published numerous books.

Dr. Smiley ... a moniker that he wears well ... is destined to become known to the world as the "go to" person if success is one of your goals in life. There truly may be no secret to success, but if there is a path then wisdom is one to follow with Dr. Smiley helping you develop your dream.

... Dr. James A. Omps, President, IUE

Preface

This dissertation is broken up into an alphabetical table of contents to allow for easier searchability. My mind works this way when I brainstorm each day, so I hope you find this helpful. I am listing the topics as if this were a book, so that if you wish to read a specific section, you can jump to it, or if this flow does not work for you, it can still be navigable.☺

Ultimately, I intend to prove several things in this dissertation.

1. The consumption of good knowledge and wisdom will always make a better entrepreneur and leader.

2. That the effort and time put into oneself to develop their ultimate 'Who' or work in progress toward the 'Who' they wish to capitalize on whether it be for financial or purpose driven.

3. That the greater the 'Who' one is up for believing in and creating, the greater the 'Why' (Purpose) one will discover is possible to achieve. This will in essence be the passion fuel that will drive one to contribution and higher order impact in the world.

4. Ultimately that when you 'Who' and 'Why' are established at a level that is awe inspiring, the 'How' will be effortless in how one achieves great results in helping others obtain abundance, solve problems and inspire hope.

5. Harmony in life is the goal, and I believe Entreprenology is a gateway to the utopian life. One through the program being available and known more mainstream. Second, that in fulfilling the program,

you further the 'Who', 'Why' and 'How' for the purpose of Planetary Peace, Power and Prosperity. And finally, when you have graduated from with this PhD, you are armed with a title that is symbolic of a person who is prophet at making a profit... which is to say a world with abundance. (See TEDx section)

Setting the intention is one of the most powerful forces we bestow. With that said, the intention of this pursuit of my doctorate in Entreprenology is as follows:

1. To accomplish a life goal

2. To become known as Dr. Smiley

3. To create a coaching process and program offered through IUE (International University of Entreprenology) that utilizes what we are doing to complete our PhD in a timely fashion

4. To collaborate on creating a marketing and sales system for IUE (International University of Entreprenology)

5. To expand the terminology Entreprenology

6. To help fund The Keep Smiling Movement through joint venture sales

7. To help life learners leverage their experiences into a PhD program

8. To bring more value to the lives of leaders and the Entreprenology program.

Table Of Contents
(Earnings and Learnings)

Introduction

"A man is but a product of his thoughts. What he thinks he becomes."
~ Mahatma Ghandi

Entreprenology is the study of cumulative experience, knowledge, and wisdom. It is an evaluation and reflection of all academically and experientially learned facets of your life. Since life is a journey of experiences, it is vital they are documented and learned from in order to enhance our abundance and happiness. This program is the key to going back and relearning what was learned, applying these lessons to our current life and most important, seeing how all these dots caused us to be who we are today... a future leader with a PhD.

The more you have lived, the more work this dissertation will be... but also the more rewarded you will be for taking the deep dive to reeducate and learn wisdom from your mistakes, successes and experiences.

Experiential learning is very vast in scope. It includes so many facets of entry to our brain, that it can be overwhelming if you do not categorize all your experiences. Once this was accomplished, it was manageable. Just remembering what your brain has digested in audible, audio books, books (bought, borrowed, lost, etc.), documentaries, eBooks, libraries on different platforms, movies, podcasts, YouTube lessons, etc... can add up to thousands of experiences you have to choose from. How relevant they are now, why you even have the book still and what books you bought and never consumed. Worse, what books you love, and can't even speak a minute about why they are vital and worthy of recommendation.

This program is the biggest examination you will have on your life... ever. When are you asked to account for everything you have experienced and what you learned from each experience you want to share. My saying 'The more I know, the more I grow; the more I grow, the more I find out how little I know. ~ Ken Rochon, Jr.

"Everybody has an Attitude… so Make it a Good One"
~ KJR

"When you keep a healthy perspective, you keep a healthy reality."
~ KJR

"In the beginning of a journey, I start as a child...
excited and naive for what I will experience and learn."
– Ken Rochon, Jr.

Profiles in Success Interview
Amplifying Hope through a Legacy of Smiles

When Ken Rochon Jr. moved from a small Midwestern town to Maryland as a teenager, he was unsure of what he wanted to do with his life. Being so close to the Nation's capital, he could smell success in the air immediately. "When I moved to Maryland, I had never felt so much opportunity in my life," Ken recalls. "I had just come from a place where there's no such thing as entre-preneurialism unless you count doing a paper route. I was working my butt off detasseling corn every summer, de-weeding the bean fields, and shoveling snow from driveways. All the jobs I had were manual labor. When I got here, I immediately saw an opportunity! You can do anything here and make a living."

Ken was only 17 at the time, but he had found not one but two successful busi-nesses within the year. One was an entertainment company, and the other was a design company. Today, the former is known as Absolute Entertainment and the latter Perfect Publishing. They are both 37 years old and still thriving.

Few teenagers would have the wherewithal to build two profitable businesses from the ground up, but Ken had a natural talent for making connections and selling his talents to customers. His father taught him that a good name is everything- in life and in business, and Ken quickly built a reputation for providing only the highest quality services. "Absolute had an average five-star rating," explains Ken. "As a result, we charged almost $1,000 more for a DJ for a wedding than anyone else in the area. Then we put that money back into customer service. By 2002, we were doing about 1,400 big weddings a year. We were the second largest DJ service in the entire region with 23 high-end accounts."

Bees contribute to more than $15 billion worth of crops every year through the act of pollination.

As big as the business got, Ken almost lost everything when an embezzlement scheme was uncovered. An employee at Absolute Entertainment had, over five years, stolen over $150,000. DJ work is seasonal, and the theft was discovered shortly before a hefty tax bill was due. Ken was shocked, but as he began to take steps to right the ship, nine of his 11 DJs left. They started competing companies of their own, and the financial situation looked bleaker than ever.

"They thought the business was going to fail and didn't see any path for recovery," Ken reflects. "But I had two people who had been with me for 20 years and were willing to stay with me as I took steps to rebuild the company. It took three years, but we rebuilt it into the company we were before. Then I went on my very first vacation!"

Ken doesn't believe in quitting, and he's quick to attribute his attitude to another of his dad's lessons. It's clear he profoundly admires his father, with whom he's become even closer as an adult. "Playing baseball at age 12, I was assigned the catcher position, which I hated," laughs Ken. "When I told my dad I was quitting, he told me he'd never sign me up for anything else again in my life! That hit me like a ton of bricks. I never quit again, and I never quit another thing for the rest of my life."

Today, Ken is CEO of the Umbrella Syndicate and Co-founder of The Keep Smiling Movement, an international nonprofit mental and dental health organization. Both forge connections between people all over the world. The Umbrella Syndicate, founded in 2010, is a marketing and PR organization that amplifies good businesses and good causes. Through a lifetime of prioritizing relationship building and networking, Ken maintains a vast Rolodex of connections to help get the word out about exciting new ventures. Umbrella Syndicate now boasts thousands of connections, including business owners, writers, influencers, musicians, speakers, models and more.

True to form, Ken did not focus first on monetizing the Syndicate; he still had his successful entertainment business supporting him financially, and he knew that step one was building a rock-solid reputation. Instead, he began by offering his services to prominent clients in exchange for sponsorships. "I volunteered," he describes. "I would find the biggest events on social media and let them know I had a large platform and could get them exposure. All I asked in return was to be listed as a senior sponsor. They would look at my page and could see it was blowing up. I was getting 35,000 visitors a week, and they could see the potential exposure they would get. I did events at the White House and worked with the Ravens and Redskins. None of it was bringing in money yet, but it was bringing massive prestige. That became the door opener."

With little income flowing into the Syndicate at its start, Ken was able to use the work he'd done for movers and shakers to attract clients. Seeing the work he'd completed to date; Ken began to get offers for paid work. "I went through lots of years of looking at deplorable income statements, but in the market, I looked like a millionaire," laughs Ken. "People thought I was a millionaire! I'm next to all these big companies, proving that I'm worth $5,000 to $10,000 a day, or $2,500 per hour in some cases. Umbrella Syndicate wasn't started to be impressive financially; it was a relationship collateral investment portfolio."

Ken loved to ask his to name the most inspiring person they knew and then connect with that person. Along the way, he was always looking for purpose. "Every day, I was praying, not to make money, but to know what I'm supposed to be doing with my life," says Ken. "It took seven years, and then this 65-year-old Jewish man hands me a card that said, 'Keep Smiling.' I couldn't stop thinking about this card and what I could do with it. I talked to him that weekend and asked if I could turn it into a global movement. He said, 'OK.' That surprised me. I thought he would think I was crazy."

The man's name was Barry Shore, and for years he'd been on a simple mission—to keep people smiling. Since 1999, he'd been carrying "Keep Smiling" cards and handing them out to everyone he met. Ken loved the card and immediately saw the potential of The Keep Smiling Movement. "There's nothing more welcoming than a smile, no matter what language you speak," observes Ken. "This was God's gift to me, to have an impact on people this way. My son loves giving cards to people; you give the card to people, and they shift mentally. We call it 'shift happens.' Give the cards out, and you'll see how people change, how they're happier. Barry knew how powerful it was, he'd printed them in about 20 languages, and now we're up to 25. I'd like to have them in every major language."

Barry's work and life have been a major inspiration to Ken. Barry, a sufferer of Guillain- Barré syndrome, a disease that attacks one's central nervous system, woke up one day at 55, completely paralyzed. "He is a bit of a miracle because only about one in 10,000 people can get some mobility afterward," explains Ken. "Barry swims two miles a day. He attributes it to his attitude and mindset. His Rabbi gave him the 'keep smiling' card when Barry was struggling mentally and physically. He walks with a staff today, but he's mobile. He gets in the water swims two miles. Tracking his miles, he will tell you that he's swum from Australia to Los Angeles by now." In the years between his injury and meeting Ken, Barry had handed out about a million cards. In less than five years, The Keep Smiling Movement has more than doubled with the loyal support of Dr. Andrea Adams-Miller, the Executive Director. "She turned my passion into a 501(c)3 nonprofit that 'Saves Lives with S.M.I.L.E.S by Creating a D.O.S.E. of H.O.P.E,'" Ken shares. "It opens countless opportunities to connect with others, sometimes personally and often professionally. The cards create smiles that invoke conversations. These conversations become motivational stories worthy of our Legacy book as they inspire readers that all is possible. These smiles, cards, conversations and books save lives, inspire hope and build a legacy. And abundance is created as a bonus."

Ken's father was undoubtedly a major influence growing up, but he credits his belated mother with his passion for a positive attitude. She always emphasized the importance of looking on the bright side of every situation. Ken's father was in the military, and the family rarely stayed in one place for more than a year or two. In fact, by the time Ken was 12, his father had been stationed in 13 different locations. The moves were rough on Ken, and often Ken would sabotage his friendships and leave his friends on bad terms when he learned they were moving. "My mother showed me the silver linings," Ken reflects. "She taught me that if you look for a problem with someone, you're going to find it. But if you look for the good in people, you always find it, too. My mom taught me how to believe in myself and other people."

Born in Rhode Island, Ken lived in Paris for two months and later in Hong Kong. When Ken's father was stationed in Vietnam, Ken and his mother moved to India to live in his paternal grandfather's home. His first memories are of New Delhi, where his grandfather taught agriculture throughout his career. He was the only white student at his school, but he recalls that he was easily accepted and never bullied. He learned to love Indian food, which he professes he could eat every day. He heard from his father in Vietnam via tape recordings sent in the mail.

The family's next stop was Germany, but in Germany, they moved between five different bases. "When I found out we were moving again, I'd just turn into the biggest jerk ever," remembers Ken. "I destroyed friendships and picked big fights. It was my way of not dealing with the pain of losing them. But my mom intervened when she saw what was happening. She taught me there was never a good reason to be negative. She always found a way to be happy."

After Germany, the family relocated to the US in a small town in Illinois. This area is where Ken spent the rest of his middle school and high school years. The adjustment to the US was huge. In Europe, Ken had, like most kids, been fascinated by soccer. He thrived on the field and excelled at the sport, but in America in the 1970s, soccer just wasn't an option. "Back in Germany, I thought I was going to be a professional soccer player," smiles Ken. "I was like a junior Pelé. I was 12 years old, playing with high school kids. I was an all-star soccer player. And then we moved."

Without soccer or any of his childhood friends, Ken spiraled into depression. It was hard adjusting to America despite the fact it was his native country. For one thing, the racism in Illinois shocked him. There was a black and white side of town, and Ken was called names for being kind to all the other kids, no matter their race. Some of the students teased him for being from Germany for coming from a foreign culture.

Finally, a friend of Ken's dad suggested that he try out for the cross country and thought that perhaps running would be a positive athletic outlet. "I hated life without soccer, and I was about two years into my depression," recalls Ken. "In my first 5k race, I killed it. I was in contention the entire race and was running with the top athletes. The high school coach was there and invited me to try out. In the 9th grade, I qualified for a spot at the state competition. I ended up being offered Captain of the Track team, Captain of Cross Country, and Captain of Indoor Track. And then my dad gets another assignment in Maryland."

His prowess at running was so sought after, all of Ken's coaches offered to let him live with them. They wanted him to remain in Illinois and complete his high school running career. Ken was also an accomplished artist and had already been awarded two art scholarships to Illinois State University. His art teacher also extended a similar invitation. But Ken knew that as important as his community had become to him, his family was more important. "I was 17, and I had to reinvent myself yet again," Ken remembers. "It was hard. But I didn't sabotage relationships this time, and I was committed to earning in Maryland what I lost in Illinois. It was the first time I had something to prove—prove that I could do it again."

Ken earned two small cash art grants to study Medical Illustration at Anne Arundel Community College. The degree was a mixture of art and science; Ken realized it was a way to earn money while embracing his love of art. "I had a love of anatomy," says Ken. "I was studying Leonardo da Vinci's anatomy drawings when I was in the second grade." His love of science, meanwhile, was spurred on by a harsh third-grade teacher, Mr. Engel. "He was strict," Ken grins. "He ran his science class like a military school. No matter how hard I worked, I couldn't get more than a C- in his class. But as demoralized as I was, when I went on to 4th, 5th, and 6th grade, I was always the top student in science all because of Mr. Engel."

Despite his love for art, Ken quickly realized that medical illustration was not at all creative. He decided he wanted to make a difference, particularly to kids in his community, finishing college with a degree in education. He knew teaching paid very little, but he enjoyed influencing young minds, and he was making money with his DJ business. His teacher's salary served as a supplement rather than his only income stream. "The idea of teaching came from my mom," Ken states. "My mom taught for 22 years before she was diagnosed with dementia."

Ken spent a few years teaching in Prince George's County before realizing that as much as he wanted to change his community for the better, the education system wasn't built for real change. "I was naïve to think I could make a difference in that system," admits Ken. "If a kid worked in my class and put forth an effort, I would give them a minimum of 70%. But the principal I worked for didn't see things the same way. His focus was to cash the check and go along to get along."

In 2005, Ken's mother was diagnosed with Alzheimer's, and he devoted himself full-time to assisting his father with her care. It was a new dimension to the relationship between father and son. "I'm the oldest, and my younger brother and sister never gave him any trouble," describes Ken. "I probably gave him 50 times more trouble than both combined! I was rebellious, and that didn't fit well with his military background. But when my mom got sick, I was the one who dropped everything. For three years, I minimized everything else I was doing to help him. My dad and I became super close because of that situation."

After his mother passed away, Ken followed through on a lifelong dream of publishing a book. "She had always wanted to be an author, and she left without getting to do that," relates Ken. "I committed to not letting that be my story. A year after she died, I published my first book, *Becoming the Perfect Networker.*"

Around the same time, Ken's future wife, Nelly, entered the picture. She was patient with Ken's devotion to his mother during her long illness, and he loved that she understood the importance of family. The couple has one son together, Kenny. "She's a rock-solid mom, wife, and homemaker," he observes. "She makes sure home is home. When I enter the door to our house, I don't bring problems or issues with me. We have rules about that. My phone gets docked, and I'm 100% present with Kenny and my wife."

The longest flight by distance is Singapore to Newark, New Jersey with a total of 9,534 miles.

Ken's commitment to family is evident in the pride he speaks about his young son's achievements. "He can be a scientist, an engineer, a leader, or anything he wants to be," Ken beams. "By age three or four, he was already doing 8th- grade problem-solving. He's learning sign language; he knows 50 flags and 50 different chemicals and their application in the world." Ken's favorite object in the world is the self- published book he and his son worked on together, Kenny's Favorite Jokes. "It's the first thing we've done together," reflects Ken. "And we are going to continue building on this foundation."

As a leader, Ken describes himself as a chameleon. He's both a visionary and a team player. He stresses the importance of democratic management—empowering rather than dictating to his teams. "I don't want to micromanage," Ken says. "I was always working for someone who told me how to do things. I'd rather just tell you to get something done and let you come up with the best way to do it."

To young people joining the working world today, Ken stresses relationships above all else. Relationships are, after all, what got Ken to where he is today, which is part of his reputation. "You have to build partnerships," reflects Ken. "And you have to learn how to bet. One of the defining moments of my career has been during the pandemic. I would have had 99% lost income if I didn't know how to pivot, but since my pivot, I earned my doctorate and I've done some of my best work."

That best work included the two compilation books *HOPE is DOPE* and *D.O.S.E. of HOPE.* Two multiple book editions devised to showcase inspirational stories of resilience to give others a reason to smile. "The feedback has been a beautiful thing as we have had people say that they had given up," relates Ken. "And The Keep Smiling Movement gave them the dose of hope they ed to stay positive. That result is what I desire, a world where others are inspired and motivated to be resilient while they leave a legacy. With that, their SPH increases, their 'Smiles per Hour,' and when you increase your SPH, you're happier, healthier, and more abundant."

"Personally, I have embraced the sentiment 'We Amplify Goodness,' which you will find on the back of every keep smiling card, as my mission and purpose for a living," Ken states. "What a way to live life and tip the Happiness Index. Therefore, I challenge you to test this SPH Factor phenomenon to increase your smiles and leave a legacy towards a life you love that inspires others."

– By Gordon J. Bernhardt, CFP®, AIF®
About Gordon J. Bernhardt
President and founder of Bernhardt Wealth Management and author of Profiles in Success: Inspiration from Executive Leaders in the Washington D.C. Area, Gordon provides financial planning and wealth management services to affluent individuals, families and business-owners throughout the Washington, DC area. Since establishing his firm in 1994, he and his team have been focused on providing high-quality service and independent financial advice to help clients make informed decisions about their money. For more information, visit www.BernhardtWealth.com and Gordon's Blog.

0. The Power of Zero
(The Defeatist Attitude Approach)

"Nothin' from nothin' leaves nothin'" – Billy Preston

I decided there really wasn't a point in writing a book that is predictable and offers 'nothing' to the reader that is applicable and new.

Why start with nuttin'? I suppose to make several points. First, before this chapter was written, there was not a book. And if I continued with the "Power of Zero", you would be doing something different right now than reading this sentence.

This book took 26 years to write, because I used the Power of Zero for 25 years, and didn't write a single chapter, a single paragraph, a single sentence, not even a single word! I realized it would never materialize unless I adopted a new Power.

So often we allow the "Power of Zero" to dictate our lives. We believe perhaps that we have Zero money, or Zero time... or both - and believe we will have Zero opportunity. Perhaps we believe that doing nothin' costs us nothing, but there is a huge cost ... a huge loss. Doing something instead of nothing over time makes all the difference. Otherwise the hours wasted turn into days, then into weeks, then into months, then years... and for some, a lifetime.

We all know that networking is not for everyone. And most people get into networking with dreams of instant cash and quick returns. Don't get me wrong, it's very possible, and it's successfully happened for many people. Doing networking is sales + marketing + paperwork + deposits + everything else. I

Mr. Excuse

"The Greatest Pleasure in Life is Doing what Others Say 'Can't' Be Done"
~ Unknown

More than 99.9 percent of all the animal species that have ever lived on Earth were extinct before the coming of man.

read something yesterday that said the reason why people are not successful in business, be it networking or whatever, it is because of the power of Zero:

- Laziness – Zero focus and lack of ambition
- Lack of focus – Zero goals and no hope for the future
- Lack of achievable goals – Zero self-confidence and no hope of success
- Lack of real self-confidence – Zero sense of urgency and lack of direction
- Lack of a true sense of urgency – Zero personal development and no hope of enrichment
- Lack of personal development – Zero mentorship and no hope of opportunity
- Lack of mentorship – Zero support system and lack of feedback
- Lack of a team-oriented support system – Zero persistence and no hope of achievement
- Lack of persistence and tenacity – Zero mindset and no hope of change
- Lack of a positive mindset – Zero success: Period

This book is about the Perfect Networker. The statement Nothin' from nothin' leaves nothing" is so literally true because we all start with nothing. It's a mindset that must be adopted. Many of us are doing so little to create success for ourselves and we're naturally operating within the Power of Zero. You must take time to create time to attend events; you must create time to interact; you must create time to build relationships and to follow up.

If you live inside the Power of Zero, you're admitting that you're powerless – you're admitting that you have no time to create success. The Power of Zero keeps you down; it keeps you as a spectator in life and robs you of the joy of both self-achievements in business, and personal success in your life. We all start with nothing and it's up to us to pull ourselves up.

So many people believe they have no time to offer someone else; or believe that fitting in isn't an option – or – or – and we continue to make excuses.

The mindset of the Power of Zero is a dark and negative force that keeps you a virtual slave to its destructive forces.

- I have **no** ability.
- I have **no** money.
- I have **no** time.
- I have **no**thing to offer someone else.
- I can do **no**thing to change my circumstances.

The worst part of the Power of Zero is that we start believing it is the reason we can't move forward. We buy into this excuse for having no power, and it becomes our reactionary defense, canned-line for any opportunity that comes our way. We become "Mr. Excuse" (or 'Mr. Can't') adopting non-committal words like 'try' when we feel forced to change our circumstances of success. For instance, we say, "I will try to do that for you", or "If only I had more time, or money, I probably could do this". The sooner you stop using the words 'can't' and 'try' the sooner you can replace those words with empowering words like 'can' and 'will'.

"I am getting nothing out of the Power of Zero" – Ken Rochon

If you have a company or a business, and you're not marketing that business or company, then what you're really saying is that you have no time for success – no desire to honestly succeed.

"But I have no money!" Hogwash! You have your mouth, you have your feet, you have a pen and paper. The Power of Zero is truly an attitude that will keep you in its depressive grips; that will keep you with no money or friends. The Power of Zero is the blackest of all mindsets, because like a virus, it spreads into all areas of your life.

"But I have no time!" Horse-hockey! When you say you don't have any time, you are really stating you don't want to trade time that is yielding you less, for time that could yield you more. This is sabotaging your success when you believe you cannot leverage your money or your time.

The art of rationalizing your position in life without taking responsibility for what it could be... This is The Power of Zero. If you buy into The Power of Zero, you adopt a very gloom and doom perspective on life. Why wait for life to happen and then watch opportunity after opportunity pass you by because "They are not the 'One'!"?

Applying the Power of Zero to Relationships

I find it intriguing that people can love another human being for years, and in one day throw away the relationship because of a misunderstanding, or gossip, etc.

Some people choose the inefficient route of finding new relationships they hope will be 'perfect' instead of building and repairing the relationships that already exist.

When you want to create a network of people that support and love you, then you to be the one that is the bigger person. When there is a misunderstanding, be in communication, be the one to fight for the relationship. You will thank yourself later.

I've lost some relationships in my life that I wish I could understand why they evaporated... perhaps I will never know, but I have saved many relationships through taking the advice I shared in this section.

If you truly consider the time and effort we put into building a relationship, and the little effort it takes to mend it is worth it almost every time... if for no other reason than to have closure and peace.

This applies to business practice as well. Whoever makes a mistake with re-gard to delivery of a product or service really deserves the benefit of at least an explanation of why the relationship is not working. You may be surprised that this conversation yields all kinds of rewards in the service and value of that relationship.

I met someone who was very upset with a vendor and decided they would pay for the service, but never use them again. I disagree with this decision, and recommend that you share your thoughts with anyone you are happy or upset with in a business transaction. Think of it as an opportunity to either make someone feel great about what they are doing by writing a letter of appreciation, recommending them on the PerfectNetworker site, etc. or helping them improve with constructive feedback.

When someone calls my entertainment company to complain, I am so thankful that they had the courage to share their feelings and that I have the opportunity to make it right. It may be hard to believe, but my attitude to make it right is often not the reason they called. They just wanted me to know it was not perfect, and they didn't want it to affect someone else. This is a huge opportunity to make your company better and avoid future problems.

I hear lots of people share their circumstances as if they are not in control of them. We must remember that we create our world. If we do so with the Power of Zero, we will be full of excuses instead of successes.

Realizing that everything we do or don't do is the result of a power we believe in, gives us control to decide what powers serve us and which ones do not. Remember, the past does not equal the future! This is the reason I chose to adopt a new power... the Power of One.

1. Abundance vs. Scarcity

- Too many of us are not living our dreams because we are living our fears. Les Brown
- Abundance Mentality comes from removing Scarcity from your Life.

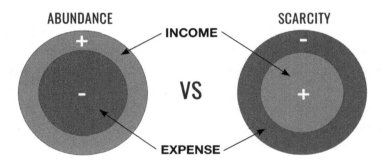

Green: – signs (Negative / Subtraction signs)
Red: + signs (Addition / Positive signs)

2. Amplifluence.com

Amplifying Influence

Mission to educate leaders to
Monetize, Publish, and Speak their Message

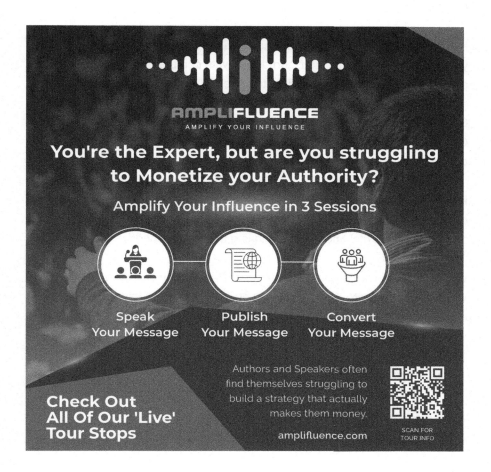

3. Attitude
(As a Man Thinketh — Creating Identity)

'Who You've Been Isn't Who You Have to Be.'
~ Unknown

Ponder this:

If a Liar tells you to do X, Y and Z and you will become very successful, and you choose to believe the Liar, and do this with complete conviction, and succeed, you have just proven the Liar to be telling the truth.

On the other hand, if a person of complete Integrity tells you to do A, B and C and you choose to not believe and dismiss this advice, but rather do the opposite, the result is failure and yet the person was telling the truth.

If you create your identity as 'athlete' and/or 'Entrepreneur Extraordinaire' and/ or 'professional business(man/woman)', and/ or 'Best Father/Mother', and/or 'Best Husband/Wife' and you live thinking this way every day.

When you are proving you will be a Great Dad or Mom, or Great Husband or Wife, or Great Athlete, Great Entrepreneur, etc., you must have a purpose and reasons that become references that reinforce the behavior and beliefs you are adopting to be true and your new reality.

- Abundance
  - Love
  - Time

- Attitude
  - Creating abundance and wellness in your life are more of a shift in being and thinking than anything else, because we are the habit and proof of who we believe we are. For instance, if you believe you are a bad person, you will do things to prove this is correct. So it is extremely vital you choose beliefs that serve you and the ones you love.
  - I chose 'I believe I am a Great Father, a Great Husband and a Great Entrepreneur'.
  - Make it a great attitude
  - Everyone has an attitude
  - Bad attitudes wear you down to nothing, good attitudes raise you to something... everything
  - Make it a great attitude

- Gratitude – ultimate reflection of appreciation for an attitude of servitude
  - For my body
    - My ears
    - My eyes
    - My kidneys
    - My tongue
    - My taste buds
  - My mind
    - My brain
    - My smile ☺
  - My family
    - My Father
    - My Mother
    - My Son
    - My Wife

> 'Don't limit your challenges; challenge your limits.'
> ~ Jerry Dunn

There are an estimated 1,000,000 species of life living in the oceans. Only 1% have been cataloged.

4. Books I've listened To or Read
(From a collection of over 2,000)

- The Bacon System by Brian Basilico (Book)
  - Distinguishing different advertising strategies and how to get desired results
  - How to use internet better to connect with new customers
  - Learning to offer services that demonstrate an ROI
- Genius... A Mosaic of One Hundred Exemplary Creative Minds (2002) by Harold Bloom
  - I add this book because it spoke to be as a book, I would to read...
  - I was wrong. I gave it away ... I should have put a post it... if you nothing but time...
- The Millionaire Booklet by Grant Cardone
  - 8 Steps to become a Millionaire
  - Step 1: Make a decision to be one
  - Step 2: Do the math 10,000 people buy $100 product
  - Step 3: Increase your income not by saving and investing. It is about increasing your income flows.
  - Step 4: Ask yourself, "Who has got my money?" Think about who you want to serve. Make a list of people who have "your" potential money that will be willing to exchange for your product or service.
  - Step 5: Stay broke. Many people tend to spend more as soon as they earn more. If you want to be a millionaire, you to get rid of the consumer mindset. Human beings perform best out of necessity

- o Step 6: Save to invest. Don't save to save. The only reason to save money is to someday invest that money.
- o Step 7: Multiply your income flows. Poor people try to replace flows of money while rich people are trying to supplement (add) flows.
- o Step 8: Repeat, Reinforce, Hyperfocus. Think big from the start, hyperfocus and repeat the steps that are laid out. People will tell you it's impossible because they can't do it themselves. Don't let this hold you back. Surround yourself with likeminded people. If you don't change your surroundings, you will not make it.
- BUY NOW ... creative marketing... by Rick Cesari, Ron Lynch with Tom Kelly (Book)
- Art of Significance by Dan Clark (Book)
- Beyond Entrepreurship by James Collins & William C. Lazier (Book)
  - o Learned the importance of laying a foundation that is scalable while a company is still small and adaptable
  - o How to set value, purpose and mission
  - o How to translate vision into day-to-day business tactics
- Invisible Selling Machine by Ryan Deiss (Book)
- The Little Red Book of Wisdom by Mark DeMoss (Book)
- Waiting for Your Cat to Bark... Persuading Customers When They Ignore Marketing by Bryan & Jeffrey Eisenberg (Book)
- The 4-Hour Workweek by Timothy Ferris (Book)
  - o Communication management
  - o Email elimination and management
  - o Learned how to manage time better
  - o Leveraging life
  - o Negotiating with clients
- Tools for Titans... The Tactics, Routines, and Habits of Billionaires, Icons, and World Class Performers by Timothy Ferris (Book)
- Tribe of Mentors... Short Life Advice from the Best in the World by Timothy Ferris (Audible)
  - o Questions to Ask Influencers to Engage them. He emphasizes that the sequence of these 11 engage even the busiest to partic-ipate. I love his choices and explanation of how and why these

questions are more advanced and intriguing to influencers and leaders who are very busy.

- 1. What is the book (or books) you've given most as a gift, and why? Or what are one to three books that have greatly influenced your life?
- 2. What purchase of $100 or less has most positively impacted your life in the last six months (or in recent memory)? My readers love specifics like brand and model, where you found it, etc.
- 3. How has a failure, or apparent failure, set you up for later success? Do you have a "favorite failure" of yours?
- 4. If you could have a gigantic billboard anywhere with anything on it — metaphorically speaking, getting a message out to millions or billions — what would it say and why? It could be a few words or a paragraph. (If helpful, it can be someone else's quote: Are there any quotes you think of often or live your life by?)
- 5. What is one of the best or most worthwhile investments you've ever made? (Could be an investment of money, time, energy, etc.)
- 6. What is an unusual habit or an absurd thing that you love?
- 7. In the last five years, what new belief, behavior, or habit has most improved your life?
- 8. What advice would you give to a smart, driven college student about to enter the "real world"? What advice should they ignore?
- 9. What are bad recommendations you hear in your profession or area of expertise?
- 10. In the last five years, what have you become better at saying no to (distractions, invitations, etc.)? What new realizations and/or approaches helped? Any other tips?
- 11. When you feel overwhelmed or unfocused, or have lost your focus temporarily, what do you do? (If helpful: What questions do you ask yourself)?

- The Courage to Change Everything (2019) (Book) by Ken D. Foster
  - o One of the best books for giving a daily plan for improvement for a life you will love.
  - o Great questions provided each page (each day) to ask and discover where your brain takes you with questions that empower

greatness within you.

- o Actions are provided to keep you in integrity toward improving your life.
- The Closers by Ben Gay III (Book)
- Blink by Malcolm Gladwell (Book)
  - o Another fascinating book for sure helping me understand how we think without thinking
  - o How choices are made in the blink of an eye that are more complicated than one would imagine.
  - o This book shares stories and phenomenon's in assessments on whether a marriage will last based on a couple of minutes of observation and how experts recognize a fake piece of art at a glance.
  - o It teaches a strategy for 'thin-slicing' filtering the very few factors that matter from an overwhelming number of variables
  - o This book was not my favorite, but certainly fed my subconscious with more fuel as to why the world works the way it does.
- David & Goliath by Malcolm Gladwell (Book)
  - o An amazing look at how the underdog has advantages because of his/her ability to use the element of surprise and how understanding the enemy is to the determent of the enemies being overconfident.
  - o He demonstrates how what is beautiful and important in the world arises from what looks like suffering and adversity.
  - o Shows that what we sometimes deem as setbacks, actually become the reason we succeed and desire to win.
- Outliers by Malcolm Gladwell (Book)
  - o I learned why success happens more often than any other theory... 10,000 hours.
  - o This lesson gave me a new way of approaching business and mindset for success. The marathon mindset.
  - o From this point on, I would give a year just to study the effect and impact of my time consistently being devoted to a focused mission with an understanding that three years would most likely be the anniversary and celebration time for 10,000 hours.
  - o I learned in doing a movement, that this is closer to 30,000

hours… or more. And the collection of all in the movement s to be closer to 100,000 hours is my theory
- Talking to Strangers by Malcolm Gladwell (Book)
- Tipping Point by Malcolm Gladwell (Book)
  - o All of Malcolm's work is important and necessary to read if possible prior to opening up a business.
  - o I think his work is the premise for failure and success as an entrepreneur.
- Outrageous Advertising that's outrageously successful by Bill Glazer (Book)
- All Marketers are Liars … The Power of Telling Authentic Stories in a Low-Trust World by Seth Godin (Book)
- Can't Hurt Me by David Goggins (Book)
  - o We only tap into about 40% of our capabilities – Called the 40% Rule
  - o Resilience and unstoppability
- The Force of Character and the Lasting Life by James Hillman (Book)
- The Soul's Code… In Search of Character and Calling by James Hillman (Book)
- Hustle Harder, Hustle Smarter by Curtis Jackson (50 Cent)
  - o Discipline at the gym… every day 1st thing
  - o No alcohol and drugs in his life
- What Would Google Do? By Jeff Jarvis (Book)
- The Power of Broken by Daymond John (Book)
- The One Thing by Gary Keller with Jay Papasan (Book)
- Cash Machine for Life by Laral Langemeier (Book)
- Think and Grow Rich for Women by Sharon Lechter (Book)
- Your Trajectory Code by Jeffrey Magee (Book)
- Hidden Energy… Tesla-inspired Inventors and a Mindful Path to Energy Abundance by Jeane Manning & Susan Manewich (Book)
  - o This is a favorite topic of mine and Jeane does an amazing job of collecting data and evidence that humankind's next leap can be one of tapping into the abundance of truly clean power, the ultimate renewable.
  - o She shares that this is more of a mindset shift than one of

technology since the technology is already proven... just the awareness this is available is another example of keeping the truth a secret.

- PIVOT... The Art and Science of Reinventing Your Career and Life by Adam Markel (Book)
- The 12 Week Year by Brian P. Moran & Michael Lennington (Book)
- Story Selling by Nick Nanton & JW Dicks (Book)
- Drive... The Surprising Truth about what Motivates Us by Daniel H. Pink (Book)
- Awesomely Simple by John Spence (Book)
- Raving Patients by Dr. Len Tau (Book)

5. Books I've Written

- The 50 Book Challenge
- The 50 Book Challenge for Entrepreneurs
- The 50 Book Challenge on Happiness
- Absolute Spin
- Art of Beauty Ebony Edition (2019)
- Art of Events (2019)
- Art of Life (2018)
  - How to create a coffee table book showing off my best work
- Art of Love (2019)
  - How to see emotion in a photo and turn it into a marketing piece
- The Art of Photobombing... Creating Engagement for Your Social Media with Dave Phillipson
  - How to take silly shots and analyze the social media viral differences when compared to serious photos
  - How to leverage photos at events to remain connected to the zany people creating these beautiful moments
  - How to be creative in naming photos for entertainment purposes
- Art of Shoes & Boots (2020)
  - How to use a book to raise money for a non-profit
  - Take a Step for Fashion and support We Will Survive Cancer
- Art of Shoes & Sneakers (2020)
- Art of Weddings (2019)

- Becoming the Perfect Networker... Succeeding 1 Connection @ a Time (2009)
  - How to be an author
  - How to avoid mistakes in self-publishing
  - How to position myself as an expert
  - How to utilize intellectual property to promote a company
- A Father Son Bond... For Building a Legacy (2016)
  - Probably one of the most important books of my life. I wrote this knowing I was starting life late as a father. I wanted my son to know my wisdom far after I am no longer here.
  - This book has 100 power concepts and words with a simple paragraph depicting the wisdom I could embark to my son.
- The Fatherhood 50 Book Challenge
- Keep Smiling Acceptance Happens (World Multi-Lingual Edition) (2019)
  - This book has the Keep Smiling cards in 24 languages and celebrates diversity and leaders representing their culture.
  - One of the most important works showing the movement as a world movement
- Kiddie Kaptions (2015)
  - Collection of photos of my son with captions that won over the hearts of all followers on Facebook
- Make a BOOK, Move a BOOK, BOOK a Sale (2015) with Sarah Coolidge, Al Granger, Keith Leon and Ann McIndoo
  - Takes on the challenges of finishing a book, marketing a book, selling a book and ultimately having the book steer readers to being future clients
- Make Your Connections Count (2011)
  - Collaborative book that I paid $3000 to be considered an expert
    - Looking back I don't see anyone who even did a 2nd book... this was considered my worst published work and certainly one that gave zero return that I can find.

- Making Friends Around the World illustrated by Tara Hannon
  - o 1st Decalingual book
  - o Anti-bullying program teaching acceptance and confidence
  - o Global thinking
  - o Each page is a spread using a phrase that connects all the languages at the same time saying the same thing with a pronunciation key to help build confidence in communication
  - o Each child character shares what their name means and what they are proud of in their country and culture
- The No-Nonsense Book on Nonsense
  - o This was a collection of a lot of years of amazing nonsense I used to entertain myself and others.
  - o The 1st book to collect 1 Star Reviews to get readers to compete with how funny and nonsensible their review was about the nonsense.
  - o Examples are varied from comedians and politicians.
  - o 'Have you ever imagined a world with no hypothetical questions' is the opening question for the reader to ponder. ☺
  - o 'Outside of the killings, DC has one of the lowest crime rates in the country' ~ Former Mayor of D.C., Marion Barry, at the National Press Club speech... the best way to show how this chapter would entertain.
- Perfect Office
- Perfect Networker... Succeeding 1 Connection @ a Time,
- Perfect Network-out Balancing a Life of Health & Wealth
- The Power of P
  - o Is a look at 12 words that start with 'P' that will get you through life in a 'P'owerful way. ☺
  - o Words are how we are programmed, so using words that empower you, would allow for a better program to be written.
  - o I believe entrepreneurs must have patience and persistence, so these words are the foundation of this book.

- o Prayer, practice, purpose, playful, etc. are other words that compliment patience and persistence to have a life you love.
- o This book is another template book that allows parents to adopt the image they wish to show off their daughter or son on the front cover and throughout the book.
- Quick Solutions to World Problems: World's Shortest Book! (2014)
  - o A comedic look at problems facing the world that if unaddressed could be the extinction of life as we know it. This book addresses solutions for addiction, discrimination and traffic (auto). See Ideology section.
  - o I gave a comedian the idea and realized it was too brilliant not to run with myself. I waited about three days to see if he would call me or take action and to my relief he did nothing.
    - This book actually is possibly my most serious books if you consider the focus is to solve world problems quickly. The back cover is the meat of the book, taking a deep mathematical and scientific dive into what the following problems are costing humanity and even the question of a future existence for humanity and this planet.
      - Addiction – Just stop it!
      - Discrimination – Just accept people!
      - Traffic – Just Go!
- Social Proof... an Actionable Business Journal (2018)

6. Books I've Published for Other Authors & Leaders

This is not going to be complete on purpose. I would say the biggest lesson I have learned in publishing the work of others is that unfortunately, I believed in their power of possibility dramatically more than they did. Most of my authors have never published before, and never published again. This data has taught me a lot about who I invest my time with to create a legacy piece. It does baffle me why leaders wouldn't attach an emphasis and focus on not just creating a legacy but marketing this legacy to create more abundance for themselves and inspire others to do the same. Of the 100+ authors I have supported to get a legacy piece published; I am only referencing at best twenty percent of them here. To take the time to write that I made a difference in their life by working with them on a book, would be an exaggeration and ironically a bigger investment in more time I have marketing them, than they have done for themselves.

I thought God's message to me was to 'Amplify the Lives of Leaders Leading with their heart to create community'. If my actions were to assume this meant marketing, publishing and sharing their inspirational story with no investment on their part, then I suppose I received what I deserved... massive debt for misunderstanding God's message. I am still in a quandary about God's message, but I think it is better translated into this: 'Amplify the Lives of Leaders Living their Mission to create a Legacy and Invest in the Partnership with the Keep Smiling Movement'. This would make it a lot more accurate, scalable and certainly enjoyable.

I have noticed that a 'Dr.' in front of someone's name is one of the best filters for partnering on a Keep Smiling book. They have already invested in the mindset of knowledge is power, publishing is legacy, marketing and social proof. And they are typically not afraid of another challenge or being in the limelight of change, leadership and being powerful.

- Keep Smiling Freedom Happens (Veterans Edition) by Rear Admiral Paul Becker, USN (Ret)
  - o This book is very powerful and contains top House of Representatives and Senators fighting for our veterans' rights
- Keep Smiling Bald, Beautiful and BOLD (4.0 Edition) by Dr. Bonita Best
- A Heart of Gold by Sharon Brown
- What Resonates by J. Charles Buck; My Own Worst Enemy by J. Charles Buck
- Keep Smiling Shift Happens (Doctor Doctor Edition) by Dr. Antoine Chevalier
  - o This is one of my most important books because it featured all the leaders I have met at events who have earned their PhD.
  - o My hope is for him to translate his story into French
- Keep Smiling Hope Happens (The Inspirational Edition) by Robert Clancy
  - o This was a very important book for me to publish because Robert is one of the most respected leaders in the spiritual space.
- Keep Smiling Shift Happens (Legacy 5.0 Edition) by David Corbin
- You Are A Supermom by Gina Fontaine
- No Ticks, Please by Dr. Nancy Fox
- Staying Alive by Dr. Vinny Leonti
- Keep Smiling Givers Gain (BNI Edition) by Dr. Ivan Misner
- Hold My Crown by Dr. Michelle Mras; Eat Drink and Be Mary by Dr. Michelle Mras; Pearls of Wisdom by Dr. Michelle Mras; It's Not Luck by Dr. Michelle Mras
- Keep Smiling Innovation Happens (The Game Changer Edition) by Aaron Murakami
  - o Some of the most brilliant astrophysicist and inventors in the world today

Sharks kill fewer than 10 people a year. In contrast, humans kill over 100 million sharks a year.

- Keep Smiling Shift Happens (Washington DC Leadership Edition) by Dr. Sammy Noumbissi
  - 1st book in the series of now over 100+
  - Gave me an introduction to the dentistry space, specifically implantology
  - I ended up working his international conferences in this study
  - My wife has been the recipient of his brilliance in implantology as a result of this relationship and ability to trade services
- Dream Life Planner by Noelle Peterson
- The Entrepreneur Mind $hift by Robert Peterson; The 50 Book Challenge for Entrepreneurs by Robert Peterson
- Anna's Journey: How many lives does one person get? By Anna Renault (2010)
  - The first book I published for someone else.
- Act of Kindness by Cherie Smith; Little Bruce Spruce by Cherie Smith; The Thirteen Year Old Sailor by Cherie Smith
- Keep Smiling Shift Happens! (Transformational Leaders Edition) by Dr. Janet Smith Warfield (2020)
  - One of the most important works because this was done over a four month stretch during COVID.
- Power of Awakening by Sally Wurr
- Keep Smiling Shift Happens (Legacy 3.0) by Wm. Paul Young (author of 'The Shack')

7. Busy Bullshit

Busy = Broke

When you tell someone, you are 'Busy', you are really stating in a sheepish manner that what they are offering you is of no value.

Busy is the Blocker to Opportunity, Relationships and Living Life. Busy is Bullshit.

8. Breakthroughs, Crisis, & Turning Points

- Overcoming fear of Being Vulnerable
- Overcoming fear of Choosing a Purpose Driven Life
- Overcoming fear of Connecting
- Overcoming fear of Failure
- Overcoming fear of Jumping out of a perfectly good plane
- Overcoming fear of Having faith
- Overcoming Losing $30K with fake investment in the medical space
- Overcoming Losing $150K with PerfectNetworker money pit
- Overcoming fear of Losing my Mom
- Overcoming fear of Loving myself
- Overcoming the Fear of Phobias ☺
- Overcoming fear of Speaking in front of crowds
- Overcoming fear of Success
- Overcoming fear of Swimming
- Overcoming fear of Trusting again
- Overcoming fear of Using a mic as an Emcee & DJ

9. Children's Books
(I was brought up on, or use as a parent)

- Flawed Dogs (2003) by Berkeley Breathed
  - Amazing true story Heidy Strüdelberg, former president of American Kennel Club and celebrated chief judge of the Westminster Dog Show.
  - She was considered the Mother Teresa of the nation's unwanted dogs: a reclusive warrior-saint of poundpups
- Archibald Frisby (1994) by Michael Chesworth
  - Is about a boy with science on the brain.
  - His mother is concerned and sends him to summer camp so he integrates with 'normal' children.
  - Camp only invigorates his ability to apply science to every experience and his curiosity to learn more.
  - He uses his science to be honored with trophies for his ability to use science to win contests, and be the hero of the last baseball game of summer.
- Sigfried's Smelly Socks (2017) by Len Foley
  - Entertaining gross way to teach Kenny to read.
- Guess How Much I Love You by Sam McBratney & Illustrated by Anita Jeram
  - Best book on unconditional love and a great father son bonding book.
  - I would read this to my son as often as I could. ;)
- 10 Minutes till Bedtime (1998) by Peggy Rathmann
  - This is the ultimate book of details and surprises
- The Little Prince (1943) by Antoine de Saint-Exupéry
  - I have read this in English and French and watched the movie many times.

- o This is one of the most creative and trippy children's book ever written.
- Where the Wild Things are (1963) by Maurice Sendak
  - o Fun imaginative story of a boy who gets in trouble and goes to where the wild things are. Time is lost and upon his return, he finds he was only gone an hour. Fun!
- Bartholomew and the Oobleck (1949) by Dr. Seuss
  - o About an ungrateful King who was never satisfied with what fell from the sky.
  - o The old watch what you ask for, you might actually get it lesson.
- Horton Hears a Who! (1954) by Dr. Seuss
  - o A story of courage and unconditional love.
  - o While all the disbelievers (every animal in the jungle) cannot detect life on a small soft clover. Horton is called to help keep this civilization safe because 'A person's a person, no matter how small.'
  - o When the clover and Horton are to be destroyed and dunked into Beezle-Nut juice, Horton inspires the Mayor of Who-ville to rally his people and only through the final addition of a voice from a little boy are they heard and saved.
- The Sneetches (1961) by Dr. Seuss
  - o The ultimate book on being grateful for what you have
  - o And the ultimate book on entrepreneur opportunities. Find people unhappy with their status and create something you can sell to give them the feeling of being better or raising their status.
- The Giving Tree (1964) by Shel Silverstein
  - o A sad but great depiction of friendship and unconditional love.
  - o However the boy appears to be the recipient of all the unconditional love and it is not clear the man ever learns or reciprocates this to the tree or the world.
- What Do You Do With A Chance? By Kobi Yamada & Illustrated by Mac Besom
  - o The third in the series of 'What do you do with an Idea? This takes another look at courage and being assertive.
  - o Every book is a means of teaching a child that life is precious, and

timing is everything
- o The uniqueness of this book is that it cleverly shows that chances are around us but if our mindset is not ready or willing to accept them, that we become blind to chances (opportunities).
- What Do You Do With An Idea? By Kobi Yamada & Illustrated by Mac Besom
  - o The ultimate book for teaching a child and even an adult what it is to be brave and be an entrepreneur.
  - o This book is almost mandatory reading for even getting your doctorate in Entreprenology.
  - o This book reflects a lot of my philosophies about what it is to change the world would be something rather scary to do and share.
  - o Be the change you wish to see in the world is more of a possibility after consuming this book.
  - o It is a clever use of words and black & white illustrations becoming color when the idea comes to light.
- What Do You Do With a Problem? By Kobi Yamada & Illustrated by Mac Besom
  - o The follow up to their Idea book and equally well done.
  - o The discovery for a child and an adult that may not realize that underneath the surface of a problem is typically an opportunity.
  - o When we avoid a problem, we don't just avoid an opportunity, we avoid responsibility and the problem does not go away, it typically grows in magnitude

"What work I have done I have done because it has been play. If it had been work, I shouldn't have done it.

Who was it who said, "Blessed is the man who has found his work"? Whoever it was he had the right idea in his mind. Mark you, he says his work--not somebody else's work. The work that is really a man's own work is play and not work at all. Cursed is the man who has found some other man's work and cannot lose it. When we talk about the great workers of the world, we really mean the great players of the world. The fellows who groan and sweat under the weary load of toil that they bear never can hope to do anything great. How can they when their souls are in a ferment of revolt against the employment of their hands and brains? The product of slavery, intellectual or physical, can never be great. ~ "A Humorist's Confession," ~ Mark Twain in The New York Times, 11/26/1905

10. Collections & Hobbies

- Book Collection
- Car Collection
- Coin Collection
- Comic Collection
- Money Collection
- Movie Collection
- Music Collection
- Philology Collection

11. College ROI

30-year net **ROI**– The amount of money earned by an individual over the course of 30 years minus the total tuition cost. Percentage of students receiving financial aid– That's loans, grants, scholarships, and other monetary rewards used to finance total education cost.

- College Facts
  - o Adjusting for inflation, it now costs twice as much to attend a four-year college than it did 25 years ago.
  - o Over a lifetime, a college graduate earns an average of $1M more than a high school grad.
- College Video
  - o Is College Still Worth It? | Patriot Act with Hasan Minhaj | Netflix
  - o https://www.youtube.com/watch?v=YytF2v7Vvw0

12. COVID
(Entrepreneurial Pivot)

- Pivot
  - 99% of your events and income are annihilated
  - 99% of your time is available to create
- Publish
  - 7 Children's books and counting
  - Diagrams… an Explanation of Life
  - Reinvent PerfectPublishing.com with New Authors, Books, Links, etc.
- Reinvent Yourself
  - PhD
  - 'Dr. Smiley'
- Renaissance
  - Publishing
  - Smartest Kid in the Room Series (mailed to you as part of inspiring others through confidence and knowledge)
- Resurrect
  - AbsoluteEntertainment.com

13. Critical Thinking & Problem

(Brain Teasers, Puzzles, Riddles... with Answers on last page)

- Brainteasers
    - 1. What is the easiest way to throw a ball, and have it stop and completely reverse direction after traveling a short distance without hitting anything?
    - 2. If you were to put a coin into an empty bottle and then insert a cork into the neck, how could you remove the coin without taking out the cork or breaking the bottle?
    - 3. Two boxers are in a boxing match (regular boxing, not kick boxing). The fight is scheduled for 12 rounds but ends after 6 rounds, after one boxer knocks out the other boxer. Yet no man throws a punch. How is this possible?
    - 4. A donkey is tied to a rope 10 feet long. Twenty feet away is a field of carrots. How does the donkey get to the carrots?
    - 5. A girl is running home. She sees a person with a mask and then runs back to where she started. Why?
    - 6. A man lies dead in an alley with a tape recorder next to him and a gun in his hand. A police officer saw him and picked up the tape recorder in hopes of determining the cause of his death. He pushes play on the tape recorder and hears the man's voice say "I'm ending my life because I went bankrupt." Followed by a gunshot. The policeman filed a homicide report instead of suicide. Why?

- 7. A man takes his car to a hotel. As soon as he reaches the hotel, he is declared bankrupt. Why?

- Riddles
  - 1. How many of each animal did Moses take on the ark?
  - 2. I am the beginning of everything, the end of everywhere. I'm the beginning of eternity, the end of time and space. What am I?
  - 3. God never sees one, kings rarely see one, you and I see them every day. What is it?
  - 4. The more you take, the more you leave behind. What are they?
  - 5. They have not flesh, nor feathers, nor scales, nor bone. Yet they have fingers and thumbs of their own. What am I?
  - 6. What word in the English language does the following: The first two letters signify a male, the first three letters signify a female, the first four letters signify a great, while the entire world signifies a great woman. What is the word?
  - 7. You have me today, Tomorrow you'll have more; As your time passes, I'm not easy to store; I don't take up space, But I'm only in one place; I am what you saw, But not what you see. What am I?
  - 8. What does man love more than life, hate more than death or mortal strife; that which contented men desire; the poor have, the rich require; the miser spends, the spendthrift saves, and all men carry to their graves?
  - 9. Can you think of a triumphant adverb that contains double 'C', double 'S', and double 'L'? Now thing of a second one that is the opposite.
  - 10. What can you keep after giving it to someone?
  - 11. What is the only letter in the alphabet with more than one syllable?

Kenny's 2nd book after his Joke book came out was appropriately 'Kenny's Favorite Riddles'. Unlike the Joke book that was designed to make him an author on Amazon, and a more confident comedian/humorist, this book was to teach him how to think and be witty. There are over 100 of our favorite riddles in this book, and these are a couple of my favorites. The book is in the box you received with all the legacy pieces created thus far in my life.

"Live as if you were to die tomorrow. Learn as if you were to live forever."
~ Mahatma Ghandi

"If today were the last day of my life, would
I want to do what I am about to do today?"
~ Steve Jobs

14. Death & Immortality

This is an important part of my dissertation, because it is the belief system that what we do in our lifetime has a time limit. Get started and don't ever believe it is too late to make a difference. I would never have imagined I would be approaching sixty in my life when I decided to finally earn my PhD. But then again, I wouldn't have predicted COVID either. Another example of what you do with a problem (or an opportunity).

- Father Son Bond
    - Death (page 30) 'Son, since death is part of life, one day I won't be here and the most important gift I will leave behind are the words on these pages. I am writing to you because I want you to always have my words. A wise man shared with me the way to really live life is to live it like it is your last year.

15. Desiderata

GO PLACIDLY amid the noise and the haste, and remember what peace there may be in silence. As far as possible, without surrender, be on good terms with all persons.

Speak your truth quietly and clearly; and listen to others, even to the dull and the ignorant; they too have their story.

Avoid loud and aggressive persons; they are vexatious to the spirit. If you compare yourself with others, you may become vain or bitter, for always there will be greater and lesser persons than yourself.

Enjoy your achievements as well as your plans. Keep interested in your own career, however humble; it is a real possession in the changing fortunes of time.

Exercise caution in your business affairs, for the world is full of trickery. But let this not blind you to what virtue there is; many persons strive for high ideals, and everywhere life is full of heroism.

Be yourself. Especially do not feign affection. Neither be cynical about love; for in the face of all aridity and disenchantment, it is as perennial as the grass.

Take kindly the counsel of the years, gracefully surrendering the things of youth.

Nurture strength of spirit to shield you in sudden misfortune. But do not distress yourself with dark imaginings. Many fears are born of fatigue and loneliness.

Beyond a wholesome discipline, be gentle with yourself. You are a child of the universe no less than the trees and the stars; you have a right to be here.

And whether or not it is clear to you, no doubt the universe is unfolding as it should. Therefore be at peace with God, whatever you conceive Him to be. And whatever your labors and aspirations, in the noisy confusion of life, keep peace in your soul. With all its sham, drudgery and broken dreams, it is still a beautiful world. Be cheerful. Strive to be happy.

By Max Ehrmann © 1927

Leonardo da Vinci's 'Mona Lisa' wasn't famous until it was stolen from the Louvre in 1911.

16. Diagrams of Life

THE BELIEF & SUCCESS CYCLE

- Belief - Higher the Belief, the higher the potential you can tap into
- Potential - Higher the Potential you tap into, the higher the action you will take
- Action – The more actions you take will ultimately increase your results
- Results – The better the results, the more it anchors your belief and future confidence

D.I.S.C. - The DiSC® model looks at a continuum of pace (activity and energy level) and a continuum of skepticism or trust.

- D (dominance)
- I (influence)
- S (steadiness)
- C (conscientiousness)

PERSONALITY ASSESSMENT TOOL: DISC CHART

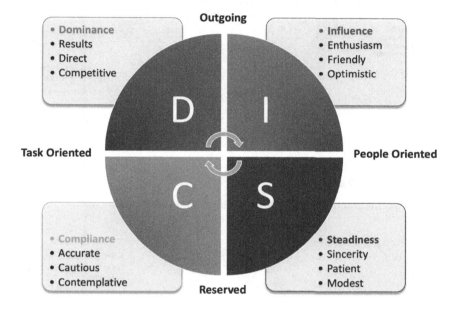

THE GOLDEN CIRCLE

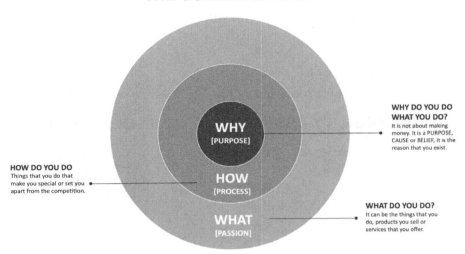

WHY DO YOU DO WHAT YOU DO?
It is not about making money. It is a PURPOSE, CAUSE or BELIEF, It is the reason that you exist.

HOW DO YOU DO
Things that you do that make you special or set you apart from the competition.

WHAT DO YOU DO?
It can be the things that you do, products you sell or services that you offer.

IKIGAI DIAGRAM

- 'iki meaning life and 'gai' meaning value or worth

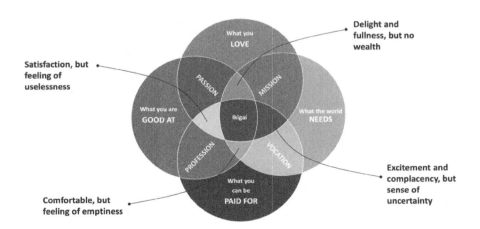

Delight and fullness, but no wealth

Satisfaction, but feeling of uselessness

Excitement and complacency, but sense of uncertainty

Comfortable, but feeling of emptiness

SMILE CYCLE

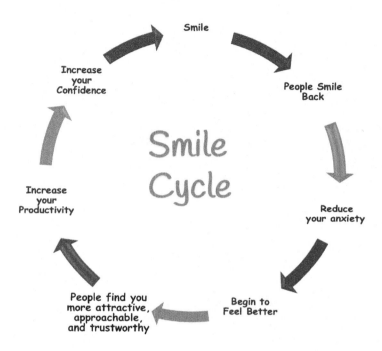

TIME MANAGEMENT MATRIX developed by Dwight Eisenhower

By the time you reach 50 years of age, you will have walked approximately 75.000 miles.

THE UNATTAINABLE TRIANGLE

You can have only 2 of 3 sides

Starbucks
Low Price
Hi Quality
(not high speed)

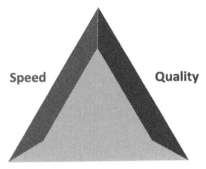

US Postal Service
Low Price
Hi Quality
(not high speed)

Speed

Quality

Price(Low)

McDonalds
Low Price
Hi Quality
(not high speed)

17. Documentaries

- 13th (2016)
- 20 Feet From Stardom (2013)
- The Act of Killing (2013)
  - Jagal meaning 'Butcher' is about the individuals who participated in the Indonesian mass killing of 1965-66.
  - This genocide led to the killing of almost a million people, ostensibly for belonging to the local communist community.
  - Anwar and his organization are so powerful that they include government ministers who are openly involved in corruption, election rigging, and clearing people from their land for developers.
- Best of Enemies (2015)
- Blackfish (2013)
- Bowling for Columbine (2002)
- Capital in the Twenty-First Century (2019) Director Justin Pemberton
  - Based on the book Capital in the Twenty-First Century (2013) by French academic and brilliant economist Thomas Piketty with a gift for making complicated ideas accessible.
  - Focuses on wealth and income inequality in Europe and the USA since the 18th century.
  - The book is about 750 pages and hailed as a brilliant explanation for why things are, they way they are and more importantly why in a lot of cases they have to be this way.
  - 'The central thesis is on the rate of return on capital ® is greater than the rate of economic growth (g) over the long term, the result is concentration of wealth, and this unequal distribution of wealth causes social and economic instability.' (Wikipedia.org)
- Chasing Madoff (2010)
  - This film chronicles how Harry Markopolos and his associates spent ten years trying to get the U.S. Securities & Exchange Commission (SEC)

- o How difficult it was to take the proof of Bernie Madoff's Ponzi scheme was ignored because of the power and amount of damage it would do to the affluent.
- o He scammed an estimated $18 billion, or $65 billion including fake returns, from investors.
- Citizenfour (2014)
- Control Room (2004)
- Elon Musk: The Real-Life Iron Man(2018)
  - o The meteoric rise of the man transforming the way we think about travel technology through electric cars and Hyperloop, and revolutionary ideas on how we live through artificial intelligence and colonizing Mars.
- Enron: The Smartest Guys in the Room (2005)
  - o Kenneth Lay, who founded Enron in 1985.
  - o Two years after its founding, the company becomes embroiled in scandal after two traders begin betting on the oil markets, resulting in suspiciously consistent profits.
  - o Lay hires Jeffrey Skilling, a visionary who joins Enron on the condition that they use mark-to-market accounting, allowing the company to record potential profits on certain projects immediately after contracts were signed.
  - o The connections to the 41st President George H. W. Bush and his son, Texas governor and later 43rd President George W. Bush.
- Faces Places (2017)
- The Fog of War: Eleven Lessons from the Life of Robert S. McNamara (2003)
  - o Lesson #1: Empathize with your enemy.
  - o Lesson #2: Rationality will not save us.
  - o Lesson #3: There's something beyond one's self.
  - o Lesson #4: Maximize efficiency
  - o Lesson #5: Proportionality should be a guideline in war.
  - o Lesson #6: Get the data.
  - o Lesson #7: Belief and seeing are both often wrong.
  - o Lesson #8: Be prepared to reexamine your reasoning.
  - o Lesson #9: In order to do good, you may have to engage in evil.
  - o Lesson #10: Never say never.
  - o Lesson #11: You can't change human nature.

- Food, Inc. (2009)
- Generation Zero (2010)
- Holy Hell (2016)
- I am Not Your Negro (2017)
- Icarus (2017)
- The Imposter (2012)
- Inside Job (2010)
  - It begins by examining how Iceland was highly deregulated in 2000 and the privatization of its banks.
  - When Lehman Brothers went bankrupt and AIG collapsed, Iceland the rest of the world went into global recession
- Kedi (2017)
- Life Animated (2016)
- Life Itself (2014)
- Man on Wire (2012)
- March of the Penguins (2006)
- Murderball (2005)
- Project Nim (2011)
- SiCKO (2007)
- Sons of Perdition (2010)
- Spellbound (2002)
- Super Size Me (2004)
  - Spurlock is in physically above average shape according to his personal traner, and three physicians as well as a nutritionist.
  - He took it upon himself to do a 30 day McDiet and be filmed during this experiment.
  - He had to eat 3 McDonald's meals a day: breakfast, lunch & dinner.
  - He must Super Size the meal when offered but can't request
  - The documentary shares the amount of fast food locations and that America wins for the most obese people in the world. 1st place!
- TPB AFK: The Pirate Bay – Away from Keyboard (2013)
- We Are Legion: The Story of the Hacktivists
- Wordplay (2006)

18. Education Experiences

- Landmark Education
- Tony Robbins Life Mastery
- Tony Robbins Wealth Mastery

19. Education Philosophies

- Approach
  - Learning should be an adventure
  - Learning should be captured for review later
  - Learning should be cooperative and social
  - Learning should be correctable
  - Learning should be creative
  - Learning should be engaging, fun (gamify)
  - Learning should be inspiring
  - Learning should be interactive
  - Learning should be measurable
  - Learning should be relevant to life and time and age
- Bottom Line is what I had my students read and write when they chose to challenge their power to be powerful. The dissertation starts with this, as I believe it is what has guided me to complete whatever I start. See the beginning of this dissertation and reread it if you wish to refresh your memory as to how applicable it is not just to life but to a new student unaware of his or her potential... and the power of their mindset.
- Critical Thinking
- Discipline
- Hint Page
- Hypocrite
- Problem Solving
- Scientific Method
- Vocabulary
- Word Power

20. Entreprenology

If I were to define this amazing study (word), I would describe Entreprenology as the study of solving problems using critical thinking, past experiences and research to create profitable products, services and solutions.

I think my doctorate completion will help with a poster child. Perhaps this copy would create more interest. *'Ken Rochon, Jr. became Dr. Smiley thanks to IUE's doctorate program. Ken is the co-founder of the Keep Smiling Foundation and after writing and publishing almost 200 books, he was looking for a way to harness all this knowledge and share the importance of higher learning and the desire to be a lifelong student (student of Life). Ken wanted to write a book on Wisdom (Epiphanies) for his son and when he learned of IUE's doctorate program it made sense to leverage all the work he was doing to earn his doctorate, get his book on Wisdom done, and most important to him was to show his son what can be accomplished when one is determined and committed to greatness.'*

- Book – "The Art and Science of Entreprenology OR 'Entreprenology … The Study of Business Success'
  - o Father's Biography, Mission & Vision
  - o Legacy
  - o Marketing your PhD
  - o Program
  - o Value
- Coaching Program
  - o Accountability
  - o Completion
  - o Progress reports
  - o Revenue increases

- o Reviews & Testimonials
- Doctorate Commitment, Expectations
  - o Amount of hours depends on:
    - How organized you are
    - How much you already journal and have documented your knowledge
    - How much you have done as a life learner. The more you do... the more you have to account for.
- KeepSmiling Book
  - o 50 of your 200 students to send in their photo and how their PhD (and they) create abundance, hope and smiles in the world after going through your program and obtaining their PhD.
  - o Leverage and create a perception campaign based on all the PhD leaders we have already captured and have relationships with through events we have sponsored.
  - o How their life changed and abundance ensued as a result of this accolade being accomplished with a PhD.
- Marketing
- Podcast
  - o Jim and I can do some, Andrea and Pauline can do some, Jim and Pauline, etc.
  - o Capture the Wisdom and the impact this program provides.
  - o PhD Podcast... Wisdom for Winners.
  - o You must have a Doctorate to be on this show
  - o Show celebrates commitment to higher learning, higher standards and higher impact.
- Sales
  - o With a PhD Degree, you'll earn more over your lifetime than the average Master's degree holder
  - o You'll have unique career options open to you that you won't get with just a Master's
  - o Having a PhD Degree gives you the self-confidence that comes with knowing you stuck with your degree, instead of quitting
  - o Your writing skills will improve tremendously as a result of writing a Doctoral Dissertation

- By working with your committee to get your PhD Degree, you'll have better interpersonal skills
- Reference: https://finishyourthesis.com/worth-getting-your-phd-degree/
- Social Proof
- Trivia
  - First company to earn $1 billion in one year: General Motors, in 1955
  - Nabisco produces about 16 billion Oreo cookies a year at its Chicago factory alone
  - The busiest Pizza Hut in the world is in Paris, France
  - Pop-Tarts are the most popular product made by Kellogg's with more than two billion sold each year
  - Wal-Mart's annual income is nearly equal to that of Russia
- Value
  - Current is $8500
  - Proposed is $10,000 with room for sales person commission ($2000)

21. Extracurricular Activities in school
- Racquetball
- Soccer
- Indoor Track
- Outdoor Track
- Volleyball

"Success is going from failure to failure without losing your enthusiasm."
~ Abraham Lincoln

"Insanity is doing the same thing over and over again and expecting different results."
~ NOT Einstein even though he is misquoted saying this which is ironically a fail. ☺

21. Failures & School of Hard Knocks

- AbsoluteEntertainment.com – Loss of $150+K in embezzlement
  - No accounting system or accountability of accounting… checks & balances missing
    - CFO – VP was the only person to touch the deposits, bank statements and bills.
    - WORST recipe for financial disaster.
  - No business plan
  - No IT partners
  - No vetting of partners
- PerfectNetworker.com
  - No business plan
  - No IT partners
  - No vetting of partners
  - No Scalability for business or platform

22. Goals

- Business
  - Become an owner & visionary of my businesses
- Legacy
  - To publish over 1000 books
    - 100 of them being mine ☺
- Life
  - Live to 100 and see my son grow up to be a great father and leader
- Physical
  - Stay healthy and maintain vitality for a quality life experience

23. Habits

This habit will shift you going into your day as a participant, to being a leader who is proactively being powerful about how your day will create abundance, connection, positivity profitability with all you communicate and connect with.

It is important to note that a predecessor to this habit would be to go to bed when your body and mind rest and with a question on how to empower yourself the following day with either a specific outcome or problem to be solved.

Declaring your intention to the world through social media holds you to account. Enrolling another leader to be an accountability partner will certainly help you be more successful.

If you are an author or wish to be an author, this will be the optimal time to download your most creative thoughts. As a coach, leader and/or speaker, it is equally valuable to command your day with an intention that solves your biggest challenge for that day/week/month.

Since we are given 24 hours a day ... 168 hours a week. After sleeping roughly 68 of those hours, we will have about 100 hours to utilize. Intention will shift the 100 hours to be valuable gifts to invest in ourselves.

One of the best measures I have found to qualify you are achieving your best day with your intentions is to measure your SPH (Smiles Per Hour). I have found the correlation of the amount of smiles you give yourself and inspire in others to enjoy, will demonstrate your proportional success in creating the abundance and happiness you wanted that day.

Since the universe is in collusion to helping you achieve what you believe, it is import that you revisit your intention with gratitude and speaking your desire hourly if necessary.

Interviewing your heroes and learning their habits is what this book is about, taking an extra step and finding out how they set their intention (mindset) for the day will reinforce you making this habit a priority.

Finally, journaling your intentions will reinforce this habit, especially if you include role models who have a similar mission or vision you would wish to accomplish. Ultimately, documenting your intention will allow you to revisit successes and prove most valuable in your pursuit for a life you love.

- Business
  - o Become an owner & visionary of my businesses

Positive Whole Numbers

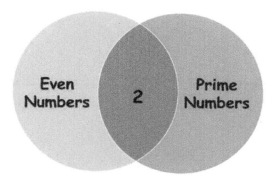

WHAT HELICOPTERS DO IN MOVIES DIAGRAM

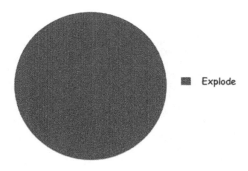

Life Finally Explained Diagram

The Complete Pac-Man Explanation Diagram

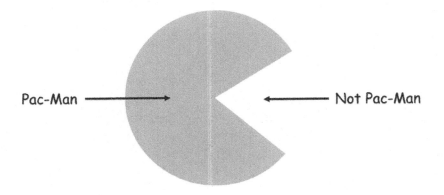

Pac-Man ⟶ ⟵ Not Pac-Man

Understanding Venn Diagrams — Not!

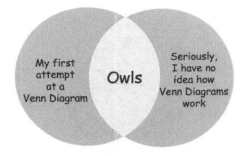

My first attempt at a Venn Diagram — Owls — Seriously, I have no idea how Venn Diagrams work

Explanation of Tic Tac Diagram

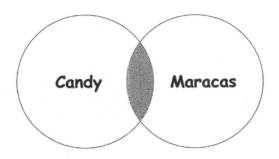

Candy — Maracas

 = Tic Tacs

THE VON VAN VENN DIAGRAM

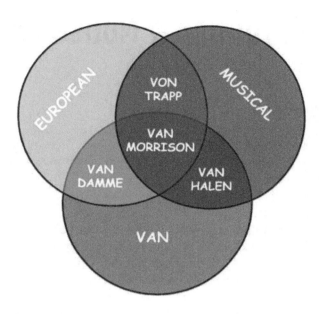

VENN DIAGRAM OF VENN DIAGRAMS

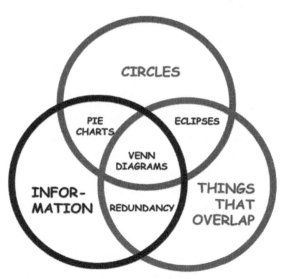

24. Humor & Nonsense

- Comedians
  - George Carlin
    - "No comment" is a comment.
    - Think of how stupid the average person is, and realize half of them are stupider than that.
    - I think I am, therefore, I am. I think.
  - Mitch Hedberg
    - I had an apartment, and I had a neighbor. And whenever he would knock on my wall, I knew he wanted me to turn my music down. And that made me angry, cause I like loud music. So when he knocked on the wall, I'd mess with his head. I'd say, "Go around! I cannot open the wall. I don't know if you have a doorknob on the other side, but over here there's nothing... it's just flat!"
    - Dogs are forever in the pushup position.
    - A fly was very close to being called a "land" because that's what it does half the time.
    - I have no problem not listening to The Temptations, which is weird.
    - I walk a lot, if I don't walk, I end up in one spot.
  - Steve Martin
    - *"Ok, I don't like to gear my material to the audience but I'd like to make an exception because I was told that there is a convention of plumbers in San Francisco this week – I understand about 30 of them came down to the show tonight – so before I came out I worked-up a joke especially for the plumbers. Those of you who aren't plumbers probably won't get this and won't think it's funny, but I think those of you who are plumbers will really enjoy this... "This lawn supervisor was out on a sprinkler maintenance job and he started working on a Findlay sprinkler head with a Langstrom 7☒ gangly wrench. Just then, this little apprentice leaned over and said, "You can't*

> *work on a Findlay sprinkler head with a Langstrom 7" wrench."*
> *Well this infuriated the supervisor, so he went and got Volume*
> *14 of the Kinsley manual, and he reads to him and says, "The*
> *Langstrom 7" wrench can be used with the Findlay sprocket."*
> *Just then, the little apprentice leaned over and said, "It says*
> *sprocket not socket!" "Were these plumbers supposed to be*
> *here this show...?*

- o Steven Wright
  - Right now I'm having amnesia and deja vu at the same time.
  - I went to a restaurant that serves "breakfast at any time". So I ordered French Toast during the Renaissance.
  - A clear conscience is usually the sign of a bad memory.
  - I woke up one morning, and all of my stuff had been stolen and replaced by exact duplicates.
  - A lot of people are afraid of heights. Not me, I'm afraid of widths.
  - I intend to live forever. So far, so good.
  - I went to a general store. They wouldn't let me buy anything specifically.
  - Borrow money from pessimists-they don't expect it back.
  - If you think nobody cares about you, try missing a couple of payments.
  - When I get real bored, I like to drive downtown and get a great parking spot, then sit in my car and count how many people ask me if I'm leaving.
  - Why do psychics have to ask you for your name?
  - It's a small world, but I wouldn't want to have to paint it.
  - A friend of mine once sent me a post card with a picture of the entire planet Earth taken from space. On the back it said, "Wish you were here."
  - Everywhere is walking distance if you have the time.
  - You can't have everything. Where would you put it?
- Bumper Stickers
  - o Beauty is in the eye of the beer holder
  - o Clones are people too.
  - o Dyslexics of the world, Untie!
  - o Shin – Device for finding furniture in the dark
- Nonsense
  - o If there is an exception to every rule, then is there an exception to

this rule? ~ Ken Rochon, Jr.

o Always... no never use absolutes since they are always inaccurate ~ Ken Rochon, Jr.

o I don't mean to brag, but I am the most humblest person you will ever meet.

o The only thing consistent about life is how inconsistent it is ~ Ken Rochon, Jr.

o The only thing we have in common is that we are all unique ~ Ken Rochon, Jr. *

o I have a consultant company that specializes in sustainability, but it is not sustainable, so we went out of business ~ Ken Rochon, Jr.

o "There's an old saying in Tennessee—I know it's in Texas, probably in Tennessee—that says, fool me once, shame on—shame on you. Fool me—you can't get fooled again." –Nashville, Tenn., Sept. 17, 2002

o The most foolish thing I have ever written is this. ~~ Ken Rochon, Jr.

o Next to being humble, narcissism is absolutely the best quality I love about myself. ~ Ken Rochon, Jr.

o If you tell someone you lie all the time, are you telling the truth? ~ Ken Rochon, Jr.

o If you are positive you are a negative person, does that make you an optimistic pessimist? ~ Ken Rochon, Jr.

o Everybody is looking for a positive quote to inspire themselves with, so I wrote this just for that purpose ~ Ken Rochon, Jr.

o I remember everything except for what I forget ~ Ken Rochon, Jr.

o If I had some bread right now, I would have a ham sandwich, if I had some ham.

o Tell a stranger "I never met a stranger I knew."

o I can resist anything except temptation

o No sense being pessimistic. It wouldn't work anyway.

- Nonsense Questions?

o Why is 'abbreviation' such a long word?

o Why do we sing "Take me out to the ball game" when we're already there?

- Why do they call it a 'building'? Why isn't it a 'built'?
- If you tied buttered toast face up on the back of a cat and dropped it from a height, what would happen?
- Why is it called 'after dark' when it is 'after light'?
- Before drawing boards, what did they go back to?
- Why do you drive on parkways and park on driveways?
- Why is 'dyslexic' so hard to spell?
- What is a 'free' gift? Aren't all gifts free?
- Why don't you ever hear of grunted employees?
- Why does the word "lisp" have an "s" in it?
- Why is 'monosyllabic' such a long word?
- Why isn't phonetic spelled the way it sounds?
- What was the best thing before sliced bread?
- What's another word for synonym?
- Why is the third hand on the watch called the 'second hand'?
- If a vegetarians eats vegetables, what does a humanitarian eat?
- Why is verb a noun?
- Why do we say something is out of whack? What is a whack?

"To try to make the world in some way better than you found it is to have a noble motive in life."
~ Andrew Carnegie

"Always... No, NEVER type something that doesn't make sense nor needs to be read."
~ Ken Rochon

25. Ideology

- Abundance
  - Is the ability to live in contentment and joy with what you have as a blessing
- Death
  - 'A Father Son Bond ... For Building a Legacy' was written for one reason, to make my mind and thoughts immortal. This was the ultimate gift I gave my son and the following text is the page that inspired the other 99 pearls of wisdom.
  - 'Son, since death is part of life, one day I won't be here and the most important gift I will leave behind are the words on these pages. I am writing to you because I want you to always have my words. A wise man shared with me the way to really live life is to live it like it is your last year.' ~ Page 30
- Discrimination
  - My Quick Book to World Solutions was made with addressing how we must resolve the issue of discrimination and inequality.
  - We can go back to the beginning of time and learn Bullying, gossip, inequality, and judging are just some forms of discrimination that has held back mankind. The reason we argue, fight and go to war is because we don't know how to appreciate differences. This book takes on a problem that if unsolved could cause the extinction of our species.
  - Travel is the ultimate cure discrimination
- Life
- Love
- Purpose

26. K3... Kenneth James Rochon, III lives on God Willing

The ultimate gift, sacrifice and Miracle

My wife had multiple miscarriages, and our last Invitro attempt would be our 3rd and final... insurance would not cover anymore, her age of almost 40 years knocked us out of consideration for insurance consideration.

I told my wife if she would not pray all day, and shift into positivity, that I was not interested in a 3rd miscarriage.

This is page one of a book I published about balancing wealth and wellness... The Perfect Network-Out. The following is a graphic depiction of the experience... and it can not be stated enough this was one of the toughest days of my life... I could have lost both...

On Flag Day, June 14th, 2013, my baby boy came into the world (on Father's Day weekend). He was blue! This was not a good sign. My wife was leaning up waiting to hear the anticipated cry of life and was becoming more and more anxious. She asked me why he wasn't crying, and I gulped and assured her everything was fine... I was hoping, praying and pleading for what I was witnessing to change quickly. It was probably the longest 3 minutes of my life.

Kenny cried and we both exhaled and knew that our long journey of five years trying to have a family was finally a reality. It was the best Father's Day gift I could have asked for. He was born on Flag Day (June 14th) and that gave me a day of rest to enjoy Father's Day with my new son.

My wife and I had wanted children literally since we were children. So this was a long awaited fulfillment of a dream. When we learned that Nelly was pregnant yet again, we did something different. We made sure all our thoughts surrounding this baby would be positive. That included all of our thoughts about life, people… everything. At every meal and before bed, we prayed for his health. We were committed to this miracle, and having a child would be the blessing we would experience in positivity.

It really didn't take long for me realize that I ed to take very good care of myself if I wanted to be a part of my son's life through his adulthood.

As a Man Thinketh – Creating Identity

Creating abundance and wellness in your life are more of a shift in being and thinking than anything else, because we are the habit and proof of who we believe we are. For instance, if you believe you are a bad person, you will do things to prove this is correct. So it is extremely vital you choose beliefs that serve you and the ones you love.

I chose 'I believe I am a Great Father, a Great Husband and a Great Entrepreneur'.

Ponder this:

If a Liar tells you to do X, Y and Z and you will become very successful, and you choose to believe the Liar, and do this with complete conviction, and succeed, you have just proven the Liar to be telling the truth.

On the other hand, if a person of complete Integrity tells you to do A, B and C and you choose to not believe and dismiss this advice, but rather do the opposite, the result is failure and yet the person was telling the truth.

If you create your identity as 'athlete' and/or 'Entrepreneur Extraordinaire' and/or 'professional business(man/woman)', and/ or 'Best Father/Mother', and/or 'Best Husband/Wife' and you live thinking this way every day.

When you are proving you will be a Great Dad or Mom, or Great Husband or Wife, or Great Athlete, Great Entrepreneur, etc., you must have a purpose and reasons that become references that reinforce the behavior and beliefs you are adopting to be true and your new reality.

Habits are wonderful when they are good habits. When they are bad habits they require a marathon of time to forget. The younger we are the easier it is to break a bad habit because the mind has not been programmed to associate the habit with our identity.

> Happiness is when what you think, what you say,
> and what you do are in harmony.
> ~ Mahatma Ghandi

- Kenny's Favorite Jokes... CracKen You Up with my son Kenny (K3)
  - A book that teaches my son and other children to be entertaining
  - Children that can tell jokes gain confidence
  - Children that tell jokes learn the importance of timing
  - Children learn that practicing telling jokes help with the humor impact
- Kenny's Favorite Riddles (2020)
  - Riddles teach critical thinking and problem solving.
  - Unlike his other books, the answers are in the back.
- Kenny's Favorite Things (2017)
  - Teaching my son what behaviors he does or doesn't do that are my favorite
  - When a daughter or son has a book dedicated and written about them, it demonstrates pride.
  - Complimenting the behavior of cleanliness, courtesy, ingenuity, politeness, etc. the child is being programmed that this is acceptable, preferred behavior that will help them win in life.

27. TheKeepSmilingMovement.com

The most important purpose I am creating in my life. The mission is to honor leaders who lead with their heart and create community and inspire a D.O.S.E. of Hope. My ultimate Kentribution to the world... my Legacy of Love... Dr. Smiley ☺

- D.O.S.E. (in attached Diagrams)
  - Dopamine
  - Oxytocin
  - Serotonin
  - Endorphins
    - Arabic
    - Armenian
    - Bulgarian
    - Chinese - Bǎochí wéixiào (Bao-chee Wee-szchow
    - Czech
    - Dutch – Blijf Lachen (Blyze Lock-ah)
    - French – Gardez le Sourire
    - German – Weiter Lächeln
    - Hebrew
    - Hindi
    - Hungarian – Mosolyogj
    - Icelandic – Vertu Alltaf Brosandi
    - Italian – Continuare a Sorridere
    - Japanese
    - Korean
    - Persian
    - Polish
    - Portuguese – Mantenha se Sorrindo
    - Romanian – Continua sa Zimbesti
    - Russian
    - Spanish – Siga Sonriendo
    - Thai
    - Turkish – Gülümsemeye devam et
    - Vietnamese

English

Arabic

Armenian

Bangladesh

Bulgarian

Chinese

Czech

Dutch

Filipino

French

German

Greek

Hebrew

Hindi

Hungarian

Italian

Japanese

Korean

Persian

Polish

Portuguese

Russian

Spanish

Thai

Vietnamese

Urdu

The only nation whose name begins with an "A", but doesn't end in an "A" is Afghanistan.

Kenny 'K3' Rochon, III, Author and Book Series

Books That Will Change Your Child's Attitude About
Learning and Life... and The World!

Books by Kenny 'K3' and his Daddy – Dr. Ken 'Smiley' Rochon, Jr.

Book for Good Behavior and Self Esteem

Book for building confidence for entertaining, timing and causing awareness to the Power of Humor

Book for helping children approach critical thinking, problem solving and being witty

Book for Gamifying Science with facts and trivia. And understanding how relevant science is to our daily enjoyment and existence

Book for Programming Powerful Words (Patience, Persistence, Practice, Prayer, Powerful, etc.) into the Child's Mindset to Succeed

Book for Confidence in Conversation and Social Contribution

Book for teaching children about culture (cultural appreciation) and global thinking. The perfect book for anti-bullying programs

PERFECT PUBLISHING

Book for Gamifying General Knowledge and feeling confident in understanding Knowledge is Power and the More You Know, The More You Grow ... Your Abundance

28. Laws & Formulas

- Bedford's Law is the law of anomalous numbers, or the first-digit law, is an observation about the frequency distribution of leading digits in many real-life sets of numerical data. 1 appears 30.1%, 2 appears 17.6%, 3 appears 12.5%, of the time and 9 less than 5% of the time. If they occurred uniformly, they would all occur about 11.1% of the time.
- Cole's Laws
  - Thinly sliced cabbage. ☺
- Laws for Life
  - Acknowledge and accept accountability for your life.
  - Open your eyes to what anger and resentment are doing to you
  - Become one of those who 'gets it'.
  - Get clear about what you want and take your turn.
  - Learn to take charge of your life.
  - Own, rather than complain about, how people treat you.
  - Make careful decisions and then act on them.
  - Identify the filters through which you view the world.
  - Identify the payoffs that drive your behavior and that of others.
  - Get real with yourself about life and everybody in it.
- Laws of the Universe
  - Law of Divine Oneness
    - Every single atom inside of youis connected in some way, shape, or form to the rest of the universe you move through
    - Everything we do has a ripple effect and impact the collective – not just ourselves
  - Law of Vibration
    - Everything in the universe has a frequency and a vibration, nothing ever stands still, as everything is always either being pushed away or pulled toward something.
  - Law of Correspondence

- Our lives are created by the subconscious patterns we repeat every single day, and these patterns either serve us or hold us back.
  - Law of Attraction
    - This is the law of vibration in action. This law is not a punishment, but a very clear mirror of our sself-worth and mind-set.
  - Law of Inspired Action
    - This law is about taking action in order to bring what you want to fruition.
  - Law of Perpetual Transmutation of Energy
    - This law means that even the smallest action can have a profound effect. Like the seed of a mighty tree holds all its promise in its tiny shell, you have the power within you to move mountains.
  - Law of Cause and Effect
    - Also known as the law of karma.
    - Whatever you put out – good or bad, you get right back.
  - Law of Compensation
    - This law is about reaping what you sow.
    - It instills trust in us that we will be compensated for our work as long as we're open to receiving in all the many ways that the universe can deliver.
  - Law of Relativity
    - Nothing and no one is inherently good or bad.
    - Everything is a spectrum of expression, and there is more than one perspective on any situation or challenge
  - Law of Polarity
    - Everything has a polar opposite: If there's an up, there's a down.
    - If there's light, there's dark.
    - One cannot exist without the other
  - Law of Perpetual Motion
    - Everything is forever changing, and our job is to embrace the ride.
    - If life is tough and challenging, know it will change.
    - Each stage of life has tremendous gifts to offer
  - Law of Giving and Receiving
    - The energies of giving and receiving operate within all of us, and in order to create flow, they to be in balance.

'The best way to find yourself is to lose yourself in the service of others.'
~ Mahatma Gandhi

Emus and kangaroos cannot walk backward and are on the Australian coat of arms for that reason.

29. Leaders – Entrepreneurial Heroes & Legends, Influencers of Thought
(Alive & Dead)

- Doctors Who Rock
  - Dr. Reneé Starlynn Allen
  - Dr. Harbeen Arora
  - Dr. Lori Lee Barr
  - Dr. Antoine Chevalier
  - Dr. Donald Cote
  - Dr. Pauline Crawford-Omps
  - Dr. Latangela Crossfield
  - Dr. James DeMeo
  - Dr. James Dentley
  - Dr. Jere Rivera Dugenio
  - Dr. John Gray
  - Dr. Robert Haralick
  - Dr. Lydie Louis
  - Dr. Jeffrey Magee
  - Dr. Scott McComas
    - Books recommended
      - Mindset, The New Psychology of Success ~ Dr. Carol Dweck
      - Man's Search for Meaning ~ Viktor E. Frankl
      - QBQ – The Questions Behind the Question ~ John G. Miller
      - The Surrender Experiment ~ Michael Singer

- - Power of Now ~ Eckhart Tolle
  - Quotes
    - "There are three things you have full control over. Your mindset, your responses, and your effort. Everything else you have limited or no control over. So start putting your energy into the controllables." - Dr. Scott McComas
  - Wisdom
    - At it's core, the science and practice of psychology is fundamentally about creating awareness. With awareness comes choice. With choice comes control. With control comes power. Focus on creating awareness in your life. Learn to be a scientist about yourself. Observe your thoughts, emotions, and behaviors without judgment. That is the beginning of creating awareness. And above all, strive to do no harmDr. Ivan Misner
  - Dr. Derek Muller
    - Veritasium
  - Dr. Karen Perkins
  - Dr. Greg S. Reid
  - Dr. Steve Taubman
  - Dr. Janet Smith Warfield
  - Dr. Joe White
- Entrepreneurs, Heroes & Legends
  - Sir Richard Branson
  - Andrew Carnegie
  - Henry Ford
  - Napoleon Hill
    - Law of Success
    - Think & Grow Rich
  - Ron Klein
  - Og Mandino
    - Suffered from depression
    - Greatest Salesman in the World
  - Elon Musk
    - Net worth 13 Billion
    - Blastar, video game
      - Age 12 he sold the game to a magazine for $500
    - Electric Jet

- New concept that would allow 'vertical takeoff and landing electric supersonic jet'
- It would not require a long runway, so airports could be smaller.
  - Hyperloop (2013)
    - A transportation system that will allow commuters to travel between LA and San Francisco in 35 minutes or less. Faster than a commercial flight.
  - Location-specific searches (1998)
    - Created a system that initially searched for results in the geographic area closest to you.
  - SolarCity, solar-powered systems (2006)
    - Works with Tesla to create solar-powered charging stations for owners of the vehicles traveling from LA and San Francisco.
  - SpaceX, Falcon rocket (2002)
    - Reducing costs and enabling the colonization of Mars.
  - Tesla Motors, electric car
    - I own a 2013 Model S that has changed my life!
    - I only wish I had invested in this brilliant concept and man. Tesla stock has risen 3600% in the past 10 years outperforming the average stock by 10X.
  - Web-based phone calls (1997)
    - Users click a company's contact information online and then calls would be routed to the company via a call center.
  - X.com (PayPal) e-payments (1999)
  - Zip2, online city guides
    - Helping the newspaper industry put together 'city guides' for online users.
- W. Clement Stone
- Mark Twain
- Family & Friends
  - Drew Berman
  - Kim Brannan
    - Choose Love before you speak
  - Linda Meeker Rochon
- Influencers & Thought Leaders
  - Robert Clancy
  - Dan Clark

o Tim Ferris - Questions to Achieve Success you should Ask Yourself
  - What if I did the opposite for 48 hours?
  - What do I spend a silly amount of money on? How might I scratch my own itch?
  - What would I do/have/be if I had $10 million?
  - What's my real TMI (Target Monthly Income)?
  - What are the worst things that could happen? Could I get back here?
    - See "fear-setting" on page 463 in **Tools of Titans**
    - See also my TED talk on fear-setting: **tim.blog/ted**)
  - If I could only work 2 hours per week on my business, what would I do?
  - What if I let them make decisions up to $100? $500? $1,000?
    - The fix: I sent an email to all of my direct reports along the lines of "From this point forward, please don't contact me with questions about A, B, or C. I trust you.
    - If it involves less than $100, please make the decision yourself and take a note (the situation, how you handled it, what it cost) in one document, so we can review and adjust each week. Just focus on making our customers happy." I expected the worst, and guess what? Everything worked, minus a few expected hiccups here and there. I later increased the threshold to $500, then $1,000, and the "reviews" of decisions went from weekly to monthly to quarterly to—once people were polished —effectively never. This experience underscored two things for me:
      1) to get huge, good things done, you to be okay with letting the small, bad things happen and
      2) people's IQs seem to double as soon as you give them responsibility and indicate that you trust them.
  - What's the least crowded channel?
    - Book launches
      1) Blogs
  - What if I couldn't pitch my product directly?
  - What if I created my own real-world MBA?
    - See page 250 in *Tools of Titans* for full details or visit tim. blog/mba.
  - Do I to make it back the way I lost it?

- If you lose $1,000 at the blackjack table, should you try to recoup it there? Probably not
- What if I could only subtract to solve problems?
  - Instead of answering, "What should we do?" I tried first to home in on answering, "What should we simplify?"
- What might I put in place to allow me to go off the grid for 4 to 8 weeks, with no phone or email?
- Am I hunting antelope or field mice?
  - A lion is fully capable of capturing, killing, and eating a field mouse. But it turns out that the energy required to do so exceeds the caloric content of the mouse itself. So a lion that spent its day hunting and eating field mice would slowly starve to death. A lion can't live on field mice. A lion s antelope. Antelope are big animals. They take more speed and strength to capture and kill, and once killed, they provide a feast for the lion and her pride. A lion can live a long and happy life on a diet of antelope.
- Could it be that everything is fine and complete as is?
  - 5-Minute Journal (page 146 in Tools of Titans)
  - The Jar of Awesome (page 570 in Tools of Titans)
  - Thinking of "daily wins" before bed, à la Peter Diamandis (page 373 in Tools of Titans).
- What would this look like if it were easy?
- How can I throw money at this problem? How can I "waste" money to improve the quality of my life?
  - "If you've got enough money to solve the problem, you don't have the problem."
    1) In the beginning of your career, you spend time to earn money.
    2) Once you hit your stride in any capacity, you should spend money to earn time, as the latter is nonrenewable.
  - What would this look like if it were easy?
- Colin Firth, English Actor
- Jeff Hoffman
- Hasan Minhaj
  - Patriot Act
- Aaron Murakami
- Latif Nasser

- Connected
  - Bert Oliva
  - Mark Rober, Former NASA Engineer
  - Barry Shore
- Inspirational
  - Usain Bolt, Fastest Man in the World
  - Warren Buffett
  - Albert Einstein Died 4.18.55 (age 76)
  - Mahatama Gandhi
  - John F. Kennedy
  - Martin Luther King
  - Abraham Lincoln
  - Nelson Mandela
  - Lionel Messi, Soccer Superstar
  - Keanu Reeves, Actor, Philanthropists
  - Mother Teresa
  - Pele, Soccer Superstar
  - Michael Phelps, Most Olympic medals of all time
  - Marilyn vos Savant
  - Frank Shankwitz
    - Founder of Make a Wish Foundation

30. Linguistics — Global Communication to Connect

- ASL (American Sign Language)
  - I completed a semester at Howard Community College
  - I am able to sign all the letters and some of the words and phrases
- Arabic
  - I completed a semester at Howard Community College
  - I can write all the letters and lots of words but have lost my ability to speak common phrases.
- Chinese
  - I completed a semester at Howard Community College
  - I can write all the letters and lots of words but have lost my ability to speak common phrases.
- French
  - I completed a 3 week immersion course in Chambery, France
- German
  - I completed 5 years of German when I lived there from 1st grade to 5th grade
- Greek
  - I completed a semester at Howard Community College
  - I can write all the letters and lots of words but have lost my ability to speak common phrases.
- Hindi
  - I lived in India for my Kindergarten school year
  - I completed a semester at Howard Community College
  - I can write all the letters and lots of words but have lost my ability to speak common phrases.
- Russian
  - I completed a 3 week immersion in Moscow with a trip to St. Petersburg

- Spanish
  - I completed two 3 week immersions in Cuernavaca, Mexico through Howard Community College
  - I took 2 semesters at Howard Community College

ENGLISH	ARABIC	FRENCH
Hello	as-salām 'alaykum or Salam!	bon-zhoor
Welcome! (to great someone)	Marhaban	
How are you? kom-mohn tah-lay voo	kayfa ḥālik (f) / kayfa ḥālak (m)	
I'm fine, and you? voo?	Ana bikhair	bee-ehn mer-see ay
My name is	... ismee	juh mah-pell
What is your name? peh-lay voo	mā ismak/ik	kom-mohn voo-za-
Please to meet you	motasharefatun bema'refatek (f) /	motasharefon
bema'refatek (m)	on-shohn-tay	
Please	min fadlek	seel voo play
Thank you very much	shukran	Mehr-see boh-kuo
You're welcome	al'afw	duh ree-n
Excuse me (to pass by)	Alma'derah	ex-koo-zay mwah
Can You Help Me? day?	Hal beemkanek mosa'adati?	Poo-vey voo may-
Where is the ... ?	Ayna ajedu ... ?	oo es-keel ya ... ?
How Much Is This?	Kam howa thamanoh?	kel ey le pree?
Sorry lay	āsif!	zhuh swee day so
Yes/No	na'am / laa	wee / nohn
Goodbye	ma'a as-salāmah	oh ruh-vwar

ENGLISH	GERMAN	HINDI
Hello	goo-ten-taak	na-ma-ste
Welcome! (to great someone)		sva-gat
How are you?	Vee geht es see-nen?	āp kaise / kaisī hain? M/F
I'm fine, and you?	Goot, unt ee-nen?	main thik hun
My name is	ikh hai-se…	mira nam … hai
What is your name?	vee hai-sen zee?	tum-hara nam kya hai?
Please to meet you	ahn-ge-nehm / zair er-froyt	ap-se mil-kar ba-hut khushi hui
Please	bit-te	kri-pa-ya
Thank you	dahng-ke	shuk-riya
You're welcome	bit-te zair	ap-a-ka sva-gata hai
Excuse me (to pass by)	ent-SHOOL-de-gen zee	ksh-ama kee-jeeae
Can You Help Me?	ker-nen zee meer hell-fen?	tum-hem as-ir-va-da
Where is the … ?	vaw ist … ?	kyā āpa mērī madada karenge
How Much Is This?	vee feel kas-tet es?	ka-haang hay … ?
Sorry	ent-shul-di-gung	kit-ne kaa hay?
Yes/No	yaa / nian	han / nahin
Goodbye	owf vee-der zeh-en	na-ma-ste

ENGLISH	JAPANESE	RUSSIAN
Hello	ko-nee-chee-wa	pree-vee-et
Welcome! (to great someone) vat	yo-ko-so	doe-bro poh-za-loh-
How are you?	o gen-kee day-su ka	kak dee-la
I'm fine	o ka-ge-sa-ma de gen-ki day-su	hah-rah-sho
My name is	... da	mee-nyah zah-voot ...
What is your name?	o-nam-ae wa nan day-su ka?	kak vahs zah-voot?
Please to meet you	ha-jee-may-ma-shee-tay	pree-yaht-nah pahz-nah-koh-mee-tsah
Please	oh-ne-gai	pah-zhah-loo-shtah
Thank you	doe-moh ar-ee-ga-toe	spah-see-bah
You're welcome	do ee-tashi-ma-she-tay	pah-zhah-loo-shtah
Excuse me (to pass by)	shit-sur-ei shim-ass-oo	iz-vin-ee-te
Sorry	go-men na-sai	pra-stee-te
Can You Help Me?	Anata wa watashi o tasukeru koto ga dekimasu?	Vy mozhete mne pomoch?
Where is the ... ?	vaw ist ... ?	gde ... ?
How Much Is This?	vee feel kas-tet es?	skol-ka eta stoit?
Yes/No	hai / iie	dah / nyeet
Goodbye	sigh-ah-nar-ah	dah-svee-dah-nyah

ENGLISH	SPANISH	TURKISH
Hello	oh-luh	mer-ha-bah
Welcome! (to great someone)		hosh gel-din
How are you?	bee-en ven-ee-do	nah-sil-sin-ez?
I'm fine, and you?	co-mo est-as?	ee-yi-yim sa-ol, sin nah-sil-sin
My name is	bee-en	ad-im…
What is your name?	may yuhmoh …	ad-in ne?
Please to meet you	koh-moh tay yuh-muh?	mem-nun old-um
Please	moo-choh goos-toh	lut-fen
Thank you very much	por fuh-vor	te-shek-kur ee-der-im
You're welcome	gra-si-as	bir shay day-eel
Excuse me (to pass by)	day na-duh	lut-fen
Can You Help Me?	me pwe-day a-yoo-dar-may	Bana yardım edebilir misiniz?
Where is the … ?	don-de es-ta … ?	neh-reh-deh … ?
How Much Is This?	kwan-to kwes-ta?	neh kah-dahr?
Sorry	pair-doh-nah-may	ef-en-dim
Yes/No	see / non	ee-vet / hay-ear
Goodbye	uh-dee-os	goo-lay goo-lay

31. Love

- Communication
  - Choose Love when you answer the phone
  - Make a call
  - Speak
- Ultimate Power
- Weapon of Choice for Entrepreneurs ... that want to play the long game.
  - Love thy client
  - Love thy worker
  - Love thyself

32. Masterminds, Seminars & Workshops

- Author 101
- Flight Club Mastermind
- PURE JV Mastermind
- Winner's Circle Mastermind
- You Can Change the World

33 Movies

- 9 (2009) – Director Shane Acker, Cast Christopher Plummer, Martin Landau, John C. Reilly, Crispin Glover
- 12 Angry Men (1957) – Director Sidney Lumet, Cast Henry Fonda, Lee J. Cobb, Martin Balsam
- 12 Years a Slave (2013) – Director Steve McQueen, Cast Chiwetel Ejiofor, Michael Fassbender, Lupita Nyong'o, Benedict Cumberbatch, Brad Pitt, Alfie Woodard, Paul Dano, Paul Giamatti
- 13th (2016) – Director Ava duVernay, Cast Jelani Cobb, angela Davis, Henry louis Gates, Jr., Michelle Alexander
- 300 (2006) – Director Zack Snyder, Cast Gerard Butler, Lena Headey, David Wenham, Dominic West
- Ace Ventura (1994) – Director Tom Shadyac, Cast Jim Carrey, Courteney Cox, Sean Young, Tone Loc
- Act of Valor (2012) – Director Mike McCoy, Scott Waugh, Cast Roselyn Sánchez, Emilio Rivera, Gonzalo Menendez, Nestor Serrano
- American Gangster (2007) – Director Ridley Scott, Cast Denzel Washington, Russell Crowe, Chiwetel Ejiofo, Josh Brolin
- American History X (1998) – Director Tony Kaye, Cast Edward Norton, Edward Furlong, Beverly D'Angelo, Jennifer Lien
- America Psycho (2000) – Director Mary Harron, Cast, Christian Bale, Willem Dafoe, Jared Leto, Josh Lucas
- American Sniper (2014) – Director Clint Eastwood, Cast Bradley Cooper, Sienna Miller, Kyle Gallner, Cole Konis
- Animal House (1978) – Director John Landis, Cast John Belushi, Tim Matheson, John Vernon, Verna Bloom, Bruce McGill, Kevin Bacon, Donald Sutherland, Stephen Bishop
- Any Given Sunday - Director Oliver Stone, Cast, Al Pacino, Cameron Diaz, Cast Dennis Quaid, James Wood, Jamie Foxx, LL Cool J,

Matthew Modine, Jim Brown, Ann-Margret, Lauren Holly, Lawrence Taylor, Bill Bellamy, Aaron Echhart, John C. McGinley

- Apocalypse Now (1979) – Director Francis Ford Coppola, Cast Marlon Brando, Robert Duvall, Martini Sheen, Frederic Forrest, Albert Hall, Sam ABottoms, Laurence Fishburene, Dennis Hopper, G.D. Spradlin, Harrison Ford, Scott Glenn, R. Lee Ermey
- Being There (1979) – Director Hal Ashby, Cast Peter Sellers, Shirley Maclaine, Melvyn Douglas, Jack Warden
  - This movie changed my life! The reaction to simplicity, and the reward of purity.
  - A gem of gems. How people play to fit in.
- Big Fish (2003) – Director Tim Burton, Cast Ewan McGregor, Albert Finney, Billy Crudup, Jessica Lange
  - This movie is an all-time favorite and must watch to understand how I behave and think.
  - It shows a man's desire to truly give and live life and the stories he shares to inspire others to enjoy
  - It is a very interesting dynamic of a father son relationship, that is dysfunctional, but fortunately the son has the opportunity to see his father's heart, and truth before he is released from life.
- Black Hawk Down (2001)
- Blazing Saddles - Director Mel Brooks, Cast Cleavon Little, Gene Wilder
- The Blind Side (2009) – Director John Lee Hancock, Cast Sandra Bulluck, Lily Collins, Kathy Bates
- Blues Brothers (1980) – Director John Landis, Cast John Belushi, Dan Ackroyd, Cab Calloway, John Candy
- Borat (2006) – Director Larry Charles, Cast Sacha Baron Cohen, Ken Davitian, Luenell, Chester
- Braveheart (1995) – Director Mel Gibson
  - "Every man dies, not every man really lives." — William Wallace
  - One of the most important movies made to demonstrate the power we have to be a stand for humanity.
- Chariots of Fire (1981) – Director Hugh Hudson, Cast Stephen Fry, Kenneth Branagh, Ian Holm

Every December 25th, the inhabitants of the Chumbivilicas Province in Peru celebrate Takanakuy.

- o   One of the movies that inspired me to run and play.
- The Chorus (2004) – Director Christophe Barratier, Cast Gérard Jugnot, Fançois Berléand, Jean-Baptiste Maunier, Kad Merad
- Cool Hand Lukke (1967)
- Courageous (2011) – Director Alex Kendrick, Cast Jessa Duggar, Alex Kendrick, Kevin Downes
- The Da Vinci Code (2006) – Ron Howard, Cast Tom Hanks, Audrey Tautou, Jean Reno, Ian McKellen
- Dead Poets Society (1989)
  - o   Robin Williams at his best, and again a movie that inspired me to become not just a teacher, but a pedagogue committed to inspiring life long learners.
- Driving Miss Daisy (1989)
- Dumb and Dumber (1994) – Director Bobby & Peter Farrelly, Cast Jim Carrey, Jeff Daniels, Lauren Holly, Mike Starr
- Elephant Man
  - o   A movie
- Erin Brockovick (2000)
- Facing the Giants (2006) – Alex Kendrick, Cast Mark Richt, Alex Kendrick, Erin Bethea
- Ferris Bueller's Day Off (1986) – Director John Hughes, Cast Matthew Broderick, Mia Sara, Jennifer Grey, Alan Ruck
  - o   "Life moves pretty fast. If you don't stop and look around once in a while, you could miss it." ` Ferris Bueller
- A Few Good Men (1992) – Director Rob Reiner, Cast Tom Cruise, Jack Nicholson, Demi Moore, Kevin Bacon
- Fiddler on the Roof (1971)
- Forrest Gump (1994) – Director Robert Zemeckis, Cast Tom Hanks, Robin Wright, Gary Sinise
  - o   "My momma always said, 'Life is like a box of chocolates. You never know what you're gonna get." – Forrest Gump
- Friday (1995) – Director F. Gary Gray, Cast Ice Cube, Chris Tucker, Nia Long, Tommy 'Tiny' Lister
- Full Metal Jacket (1987) – Director Stanley Kubrick, Cast Matthew Modine, R. Lee Ermey, Vincent D'Onofrio, Adam Baldwin

- Gandhi (1982) – Director Richard Attenborough, Cast Ben Kingsley, John Gielgud, Rohini Hattangadi, Roshan Seth
- Gladiator (2000) – Ridley Scott, Cast Russel Crowe, Joaquin Phoenix, Oliver Reed
  - "What we do in life echoes in eternity" - Maximus
- Glengarry Glen Ross (1992) – Director James Foley, Cast Al Pachino, Jack Lemmon, Alec Baldwin, Alan Arkin
- The Godfather (1972) – Director Francis Ford Coppola, Cast Marlon Brando, Al Pacino, James Caan, Robert Duvall, Diane Deaton, Talia Shire
  - "I'm gonna make him an offer he can't refuse." – Don Corleone
- The Good, the Bad and the Ugly (1966) – Director Sergio Leone, Cast Clint Eastwood, Eli Wallach, Lee Van Cleef, Aldo Giuffre
- Good Will Hunting (1997) – Director Gus Van Sant, Cast Robin Williams, Matt Damon, Ben Affleck, Minne Driver
- Goodfellas (1990) – Director Martin Scorsese, Cast Robert De Niro, Ray Liotta, Joe Pesci
- The Green Mile (1999) – Director Frank Darabont, Cast Tom Hanks, Michael Clarke Duncan, David Morse, Bonnie Hunt
- Guess Who's Coming to Dinner (!967)
- Happy Gilmore (1996) – Director Dennis Dugan, Cast Adam Sandler, Christopher McDonald, Julie Bowen, Frances Bay
- Hoosiers (1986) – Director David Anspaugh, Cast Gene Hackman, Barabara Hershey, Dennis Hopper, Sheb Wooley
- I Can Only Imagine (2018) – Director Andrew Erwin, Jon Erwin, Cast J. Michael Finley, Cloris Leachman, Dennis Quaid
- The Illusionist (2006) – Director Neil Burger, Cast Edward Norton, Jessica Biel, Paul Giamatti, Rufus Sewell
- Inglourious Basterds (2009) – Director Quentin Tarantino, Cast Brad Pitt, Diane Kruger, Eli Roth, Mélanie Laurent
- It's a Wonderful Life (1946) – Director Frank Capra, Cast James Stewart, Donna Reed
  - "Teacher says, every time a bell rings an angel gets his wings" ~ Zuzu Bailey
- Jaws – Steven Speilberg, Cast Roy Scheider, Robert Shaw, Richard Dreyfus

Takanakuy is where men settle grudges from the past year by calling each other out and having a fistfight. Then everybody goes drinking to numb the pain and move on to a new year.

- Jerry Maguire (1996) – Director Cameron Crowe, Cast Tom Cruise, Cuba Gooding Jr., Renée Zellweger, Kelly Preston
- The King's Speech (2010) – Director Tom Hooper, Cast Colin Firth, Geoffrey Rush, Helena Bonham Carter, Derek Jacobi
- Knockaround Guys (2001) – Director Brian Koppelman, David Levien, Cast Jennifer Baxter, Dennis Hopper, Vin Diesel, Barry Pepper
- Life is Beautiful (1997) – Roberto Benigni, Cast Roberto Benigni, Nicoletta Braschi, Giorgio Cantarini, Giustino Durano
- Lincoln (2012) – Steven Spielberg, Cast Daniel Day-Lewis, Sally Field, David Strathalm, Joseph Gordon-Levitt
- Matrix (1999) – Director Andy & Lana Wachowski, Cast Keanu Reeves, Laurence Fishburne, Carrie-Anne Moss
- Million Dollar Baby (2004) – Director Clint Eastwood, Cast Hilary Swank, Clint Eastwood, Morgan Freeman, Jay Baruchel
- Natural
- Office Space (1999) – Director Mike Judge, Cast Ron Livington, Jennifer Aniston, David Herman, Ajay Naidu
- Paint Your Wagon (1969) – Director Joshua Logan, Cast Lee Marvin, Clint Eastwood, Jean Seberg, Harve Presnell
- Passion of Christ (2004) – Director Mel Gibson, Cast Monica Bellucci, Jim Caviezel, Claudia Gerini
- Platoon (1986) – Director Oliver Stone, Cast Charlie Sheen, Tom Berenger, Willem Dafoe, Keith David
- Power of One
- The Princess Bride – Director Rob Reiner, Cast Cary Elwes, Robin Wright, Mandy Patinkin
- Pulp Fiction (1994) – Director Quentin Tarantino, Cast John Travolta, Uma Thurman, Samuel L. Jackson, Bruce Willis, Ving Rhames, Lucas Black
- Rounders (1998) – Director John Dahl, Cast Matt Damon, Edward Norton, Gretchen Moi, John Malkovich
- Rudy (1993)
- Saving Private Ryan (1998) – Director Steven Speilberg, Cast Tom Hanks, Matt Damon, Edward Burns, Tom Sizemore
- Scarface (1983) – Director Brian De Palma, Cast Al Pacino, Michelle Pfeiffer, Steven Bauer, Mary Elizabeth Mastrantonio

- Seabiscuit (2003)
- The Shack (The Shawshank Redemption (1994) – Director Frank Darabont, Cast Tim Robbins, Morgan Freeman
  - "Remember Red, hope is a good thing, maybe the best of things, and no good thing ever dies." – Andy Dufresne (in letter to Red)
- Sideways (2004) – Director Alexander Payne, Cast Paul Giamatti, Thomas Haden Church, Virginia Madsen, Sandra Oh
- Sling Blade (1996) – Director Billy Bob Thornton, Cast Billy Bob Thornton, Dwight Yoakam, J.T. Walsh, John Ritter
- Slumdog Millionaire – Director Danny Boyle, Cast Dev Patel, Freida Pinto
- Stand and Deliver (1988)
- The Sound of Music – Director Robert Wise, Cast Julie Andrews, Christopher Plummer
- Unbreakable (2000) – Director M. Night Shyamalan, Cast Bruce Willis, Samuel L. Jackson, Robin Wright, Spencer Treat Clark
- Zero Effect

34. Music

I was addicted to music since I was a child.

My dad had an impressive 45 collection of 60's music that inspired me to be a future collector

Joel Whitburn, founder of Record Research, Inc. is an avid music collector that was able to monetize his hobby through the publication of music charts and the trivia to accompany how the dots of music legends were a part of a lot of success stories.

I would create art from listening to music of Blue Oyster Cult, Electric Light Orchestra, Rush, etc.

I chose music to meditate to when I wanted to channel, create, distress, escape, and feel alive.

My collection is insured for $250K... unfortunately it is better if it is burned than sold ☹
- But all legal, almost virgin vinyl

The Entrepreneurial Playlist – I have created best in art and business when I had music stimulate my mind. With that said, here is the playlist I am creating during COVID to get through the dissertation and future ideas. Meditation and Music are stimulation to the creative juices we to be inspired to succeed.
- Awake by Tycho
- Been a While by Sam Feldt
- Believe by Meek Mill
- Born to Be Yours by Kygo & Imagine Dragons
- Circles by Post Malone
- Coasted by deadmau5
- Come Alive by Hugh Jackman, Keala Settle, Daniel Everidge, Zendaya & The Greatest Showman Ensemble

- Djs Gotta Dance More by A-Trak (feat. Todd Terry)
- Dream On - Morel's Pink Noise Club Mix by Depeche Mode
- The Fatback Showdown by Bongolian
- Feel it Still by Portugal. The Man
- French Kiss (Underground Mix) by Lil' Louis & The World
- French Letter by J-walk
- From Now On by Hugh Jackman & The Greatest Showman Ensemble
- The Greatest Show by Hugh Jackman, Keala Settle, Zac Efron, Zendaya & The Greatest Showman Ensemble
- Higher Ground by ODESZA (feat. Naomi Wild)
- ily (i love you baby) by Surf Mesa [feat. Emilee]
- Intro by The xx
- Listen by Urban Species & MC Solar
- The Look of Love (Madison Park vs. Lenny B. Remix) by Nina Simone
- A Million Dreams by Ziv Zaifman, Hugh Jackman & Michelle Williams
- Natural by Imagine Dragons
- Never Enough by Loren Allred
- One Day by Koolulam
- The Other Side by Hugh Jackman & Zac Efron
- The Passenger (LaLaLa) by LUM!X, MOKABY & D.T.E & Gabry Ponte
- Pump Up the Volume (USA 12" Mix) by Colourbox (M/A/R/R/S)
- Red Lights by Tiësto
- Rewrite the Stars by Zac Efron & Zendaya
- Rockstar by Ilkay Sencan, Dynoro & Joel Gustafsson Schönborg (Post Malone)
- ROCKSTAR by DaBaby (feat. Roddy Ricch)
- Roses (Imanbek Remix) by SAINt JHN
- Sound of Violence (Main Mix) by Dennis de Laat
- Spiritual High, Pt. 3 by Moodswings, Martin Luther King, J.F.T. Hood & Amanda Vincent
- Stole the Show by Kygo (feat. Parson James)
- Supernature by Cerrone
- Take You Higher (Radio Edit) by Goodwill & Hook N Sling
- This Is Me by Keala Settle & The Greatest Showman Ensemble
- You Won't See Me Cry by B-Tribe

"The opportunity of a lifetime must be seized
within the lifetime of the opportunity."
~ Linda Ravenhill

35. Networking
(Offline & Online Platforms)

- Alignable.com
- BeeKonnected.com
- Facebook.com
- LinkedIn.com

36. Numbers

- What happened in the middle of the 20th century that will not happen again for 4,000 years?
- If you double a penny for 30 days how much will you have? How much will you have on 31 days?

MAGIC SQUARE

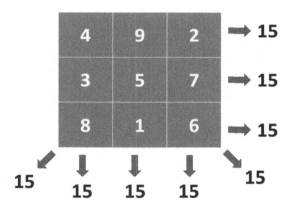

MULTIPLICATION HACK

$$97 \times 96 = 9312$$

100-97   100-96   100-7

$$3 + 4 = 7$$

X

37. Opportunities

- Are everywhere if you look
- WeddingPodcast.Love
  - o   To resurrect AbsoluteEntertainment.com

'The Secret to a Successful Partnership is to
Create Competitive Unconditional Giving.'

~ KJR

38. Partnerships — Joint Venture, Strategic, etc.

Definition
- Live•Loco•Love Studios (2017-2018)
  - Nadine Molas
  - 1st commissioned Keep Smiling book made and even for a dentist (Dr. Sammy Noumbissi
  - The studio brought the Who's Who of D.C. right to us.
  - Not profitable
  - Nadine's husband wanted it to produce money and it we did not have a business model that would consistently pay the bills.
- PerfectNetworker.com (2008-2013)
  - Glenn Garnes & Mac Cassity
  - Most costly money pit of my life
- PerfectPublishing.com – (2009-current)
  - Al Granger best partner in the world
  - Never complains and does the job that I can't do well... the details.
- Rochon, Brown & Associates Professional Disc Jockey Service
  - Tim Brown was ed to grow the company in a scalable fashion
  - Tim's strengths were systems and technology
  - Ken brought recruiting, marketing, sales, and vision
- The Red Umbrella
  - Andrea Adams-Miller, PR
  - Bank account for collaborative deals and payouts caused by the collaborative work.
  - Strategic partnership
    - Data collection

- Lead generation
- Referrals
- Union of The Red Carpet Connection & The Umbrella Syndicate to strategically work to create abundance, opportunities, streamline impact and value.
- Unofficial company without a brand, just an legal entity.

39. Personal Life Experiences
(Army Brat, Bullying, Childhood, Grandparents, Moving, Military, Relationships, Marriage, Divorce, Fatherhood, Mother Caregiving, Mother's illness & Death)

- My grandmother and uncle were published poets.
- This was the inspiration for me to become an author before I died.
- Army Brat
  - My Dad was a Signal Officer in the U.S. Army
  - My Dad did a tour in Vietnam
- Bullying
  - Because I was moving from city to city every year, I was the new kid twelve times before I was 13 years old.
  - This was my introduction of what it is to be bullied
- Childhood
  - My Dad was very busy as an Army officer and only saw him for a short period.
  - Unfortunately because I was not a well behaved boy, I was often disciplined by my Dad when he got home from work.
  - His tour to the Vietnam War was a complete and unpredictable shift in my life
    - I lived in India with my brother, mother and grandfather and his wife for the year my Dad was in Vietnam
    - I learned what it was like to be abundantly rich. We lived in a beautiful 'palace' with 9 servants.
    - The servants were there to serve, cook, protect us (from snakes)

- That year was my only year in life without chairs and silverware.
  - We ate all meals on a pillow and with our hands.
    - Divorced after a marriage with a woman with a bi-polar disorder.
    - Learned it is advisable to live with someone you 'love' for a year to make sure it will stand the test of time.
- Divorce (The Ultimate Failure)
  - My first marriage was similar to a horror movie… still could be ☺
  - I can't watch War of the Roses or Body Heat with Kathleen Turner… because my wife resembled her beauty and her temper in the movies.
  - She was bipolar which was a new experience for me… one I understand I don't wish to do again.
  - Learned it is advisable to live with someone you 'love' for a year to make sure it will stand the test of time.
- Marriage (The Ultimate Partnership)
  - Easy to divorce, difficult to stay… the ultimate statement of commitment and persistence.
  - Is it better to have a good spouse who doesn't believe in you or a bad spouse who does believe in you?
  - It is better to have a good spouse who is not capable of affection, forgiveness, and your ed love languages, or to have a bad spouse who is capable of affection, forgiveness and your ed love languages?
  - If you love your spouse, but are not in love with your spouse… is this a marriage?
  - Substitute this the word 'spouse' for 'business partner'
  - The **idiom "Behind every great man** is a **great** woman" is defined as an expression in use at least since the mid-1940s. The woman in question usually is a wife or a mother; the observation is that no **man** gets to be **"great"** in a vacuum, and some woman, somewhere, had a hand in the **man's** success.
- Military
  - Basic Camp
  - Advanced Camp
  - Airborne

The year was 1987, and I was in R.O.T.C. (Reserve Officer Training Corps) at Johns Hopkins University. I had just completed basic course and finished in the top 1%. I was awarded acceptance to Airborne School.

I accepted an offer / opportunity to attend airborne school in the Army against my Dad's wishes. I was taught for the first time I was not immortal. I suffered a 3rd degree sprain, was barely able to walk with my elephant sized ankle. My boots that would normally lace to the top and circle my leg twice with ample room for a double knot, were reduced to tying my boot two eyelids lower and just barely enoough to do a double knot. I was encouraged by my colleagues to continue to complete the school and they would cover for me so I wouldn't have to put weight on my ankle except for the remaining four jumps.

I ended up with two concussions and taking really bad hits to my hip and back to avoid landing on this ankle again. I later learned over 4 officers had been paralyzed from attending this school. I had one more jump to make and was concerned I was going against God's will. I prayed I would live through this test... I did.

But I wasn't able to run for over a year. Being a past state runner and having this part of my regiment drove me crazy that it was being removed from my life. Every time I ran, my ankle would blow up like a balloon.

Every month I tried, and same result. I would wait three months and again same result. I didn't see an end to this and was very depressed. My mom knew a holistic healer who was willing to see me. She was extremely insightful and located all my past injuries by sensing heat and turmoil in that region of the body. I had two significant injuries prior to my ankle and she located both of them with only hovering her healing hands above these areas.

She put her hands above my ankle and asked me to release the energy by thinking of something and focusing on this image. I thought of a lion roaring and it became a fire breathing dragon. What is interesting is when I was thinking of the lion, my ankle heated up and she felt this and asked me to focus as a feeling of warmth and sweating happened in that vicinity. I broke my concentration and she immediately sensed this and said to refocus again. I saw a dragon and it was exhaling massive flames. That second she said 'Great, keep focused' It was as if my ankle was a toothpaste tube being squeezed and all the toothpaste was oozing out of the top. She worked on this image for about five minutes. I was blown away when she allowed me to get up and get dressed and I saw my ankle completely normal. Like the other I couldn't tell the difference. She informed me I would only one more treatment.

I was blown away. I ran the following day against her wishes and the ankle was stronger but it did revert to blowing up to about half the size it did before.

After the final treatment a couple weeks later, I never ed to return again. I was healed and allowed my ankle an extra couple of weeks to take in this new energy force. I ran, and was so happy that my ankle supported my weight and I was back.

She suggested that my Dad and my apprehension to go to Airborne school caused the injury to not only happen but to persist. She released the energy and I learned the power of holistic healing. I was a believer.

She will never know what a difference she made and through this dissertation I hope to find her and thank her.

- o   Transportation
- •   Parenting (The Most Important Partnership)
  - o   One of the phenoms of life… that how you parent causes, inspires and legalizes your life.
  - o   I have relearned everything like a dissertation in order to filter what is best for my son to experience and learn.

"My most brilliant achievement was my ability to be able to persuade my wife to marry me." – Winston Churchill

'A long and unhappy marriage is not a successful marriage'

'The moment that you start to wonder if you deserve better, you do'

'The worst part about being in a bad marriage isn't the lack of sex, it's the lack of communication and the feeling of being alone even though you're legally tied down with someone'

"When a man opens a car door for his wife, it's either a new car or a new wife." – Prince Philip

"My most brilliant achievement was my ability to be able to persuade my wife to marry me." – Winston Churchill

"Marriage lets you annoy one special person for the rest of your life." – Unknown

"Experts on romance say for a happy marriage there has to be more than a passionate love. For a lasting union, they insist, there must be a genuine liking for each other. Which, in my book, is a good definition for friendship." – Marilyn Monroe

"A successful marriage requires falling in love many times, always with the same person." – Mignon McLaughlin

"Never marry the one you can live with, marry the one you cannot live without." – Unknown

'If you are in a bad marriage, own that you are the reason why, and change it!' ~ Ken Rochon, Jr.

"Work like you don't the money, love like you've never been hurt and dance like no one is watching." ~ Randall G Leighton

"When I let go of what I am, I become what I might be." ~ Lao Tzu

40. Philosophies of Life

- A, B, C's of Abundance, Happiness and Success
  - A – Attitude is Inspiring, Positive, and Uplifting
  - B – Believe in Yourself Becoming Your Future Self Uplifting
  - C – Commit Completely and Consistently for the Distance you Must Go in Order to Have A and B Realized.
- Busy
  - A – Attitude is Inspiring, Positive, and Uplifting
  - B – Believe in Yourself Becoming Your Future Self Uplifting
  - C – Commit Completely and Consistently for the Distance you Must Go in Order to Have A and B Realized.
- Trust
  - Do you trust someone because they have done you no wrong?
    - 100% trust given
      - A hopeful approach to forgiveness and possibility
    - I find trusting people your intuition says are safe will lead you to a more efficient partnership of abundance and co-creation
  - Do you make people earn trust?
    - 0% trust given
      - 1 mistake mentality, go back to go or be banished.
    - This approach punishes people, and basically states you are guilty of not being trustworthy until you can prove otherwise.

41. Psychology – Understanding the Human Condition

- Sales
  - Assumptive sales are one of the best means of asserting confidence and connection to a conclusion of working together.
  - People buy from people they like and trust… so be likeable and trustworthy. Simple.
  - Zig Ziglar the ultimate book on sales in my opinion

"The effect you have on others is the most valuable currency there is."
~ Jim Carrey

"Too many of us are not living our dreams because we are living our fears."
~ Les Brown

42. Podcast

- Amplified with Ken Rochon
  - Lydie Livolsi – 2020 7 views
    - https://www.youtube.com/watch?v=DJ_FjJuJq4Y
- Dancing With Words, Dancing With Wisdom – 2020 1 views (58 min.)
  - https://www.youtube.com/watch?v=ENjcrUH-F0o
- Nice Guys on Business (Episode 187) – 2017 – 9 views
  - Using Your Business Umbrella for the Consumer's Rain
  - https://www.youtube.com/watch?v=PlJ8jRQt27o
- V. Helena
  - Celebrity Photographer & Author Ken Rochon is in THE HAVEN
  - https://www.youtube.com/watch?v=JUwDakQIHHs

43. Power

- Power of 1
  - Everyone has the power to change the world
  - Do you choose to acknowledge, embrace and exercise this power?
- Power of 2 (Partnership)
  - Secret to having a great partnership is to have two parties both agree to compete to give more than the other unconditionally
- Power of 3 (3rd Party Endorsement)
  - Combine people through text to witness this Power
  - Want referrals? Earn them with giving them
- Power of 4 (4th Dimension - Time)
  - 24 hours a day (86,400 seconds)
  - 168 hours a week... we are asleep for 68 of them... leaving exactly 100
    - Count your hours... and you will have the percent of:
      - Productivity
      - Waste
  - How we use them or waste them has a huge impact on our wealth and wellness
- Power of 5 (Your 5 closest friends)
  - You are the product of the 5 people you hang with
    - Are they authors?
    - Are they entrepreneurs?
    - Are they leaders?
    - Are they positive?
    - Are they purpose-driven?
- Power of Belief
  - What you believe you achieve
  - You can not help but prove yourself right, so make sure your

beliefs serve you and those you love
- Power of Consistency
  - Ultimately defines your integrity and position in the hierarchy of your space.
- Power of Frequency
  - The more you show up, the more top of mind you become
  - The amount of times you connect with your top 100 customers, friends, and influencers
  - The phenomenon of being on a podcast a day
  - Reading a book a week / month
  - Writing a book a year
- Power of Gratitude
  - The Universe gives more what you give thanks more
  - My son is asked to give thanks every day in his journal at at one meal
  - He typically hears me give thanks for health, him, home and something I want to attract
- Power of Legacy
  - Authorship calls you to be a new version of you... a much better one
- Power of a Smile
  - The reason the KSM (TheKeepSmilingMovement.com) was created
  - Smile is the universal expression of love (acceptance, peace, positivity)
- Power of Variables
  - Add a variable to an equation and it could destroy and launch you to another stratosphere.
  - Find the variables that determine your results and success
  - There is a relationship to the variables and the amount of reviews you receive.
  - Variable A = 10 and that is the highest you can achieve
  - Variable B = 10 and now you can achieve up to 100
  - Variable C = 10 and now you can achieve up to 1000

44. 5 Publishing and Leaving a Legacy AND Abundance

https://rb.gy/drtfdc

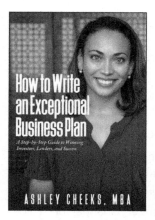

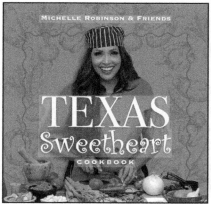
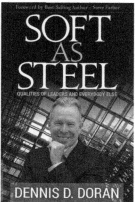

45. Purpose Driven Life

- Perfect Publishing
  - Create legacy for me and other leaders
  - Market the legacy item for me and other leaders
  - Social Proof the legacy item with photography and social media for me and the our clients.
  - Connect events to books
  - Launch books with influencers and viral campaigns
- The Umbrella Syndicate (TUS)
  - Amplify and promote events to partner and create brand awareness for TUS, client, host, sponsors.
  - Develop six complimentary media branches that worked in harmony to propel leaders into the limelight
  - Disrupt the photography industry with speed, viral marketing, and social proof
- Amplified with Ken Rochon on the Influencer Channel on Voice America
- Live•Loco•Love Studios
  - Location to capture leaders and publish them in Keep Smiling books
  - Dr. Sammy Noumbissi becomes the 1st recipient of a local Keep Smiling book.
- The Keep Smiling Movement
  - Capture smiles and post
  - Publish smiles to promote the movement
  - Create a scalable templated system to afford all leaders the opportunity to share their inspiring story and position them as a leader worthy of support

46. Questions
(That Empower Greatness for Entrepreneurs & Leaders)

- "How can I project my brilliance into the world more?"
- "How will I celebrate when my most pressing challenge is complete?"
- "How can I increase my gratitude?"
- "How will I simply my life?"
- "How can I live my highest values each day?"
- "What can I become more aware of?"
- "What am I truly grateful for?"
- "What are three steps I can take to expand my influence?"
- "What has it cost me to keep my negative habits?"
- "What is a personality trait I will change or improve upon?
- "What am I pretending not to see?"
- "What will I stop doing that will create more ease in my life?"
- "What is my highest purpose for being alive?"
- "What can I let go of thinking that will forever change the way I perceive success?
- "Who am I becoming because of pursuing my highest purpose?"
- "Who am I evolving into as a I increase my service to others?"

47. Quotes

- "You can't use up creativity. The more you use, the more you have." ~ Maya Angelou
- "Waste no more time arguing what a good man should be. Be one." ~ Marcus Aurelius
- "Humility does not mean you think less of yourself. It means you think of yourself less." ~ Kenneth Blanchard
- "My sense of my importance to myself is tremendous. I am all I have, to work with, to play with, to suffer and enjoy. It is not the eyes of others that I am wary of, but my own." ~ Noel Coward
- "Happiness is not something ready made. It comes from your own actions." ~ The Dalai Lama
- "The way to get started is to quit talking and begin doing" ~ Walt Disney
- "Impact happens in harmony when patience and persistence co-exist." ~ Dr. Smiley ☺
- "It is very sad to me that some people are so intent on leaving their mark on the world that they don't care if that mark is a scar." ~ John Green
- "Never mistake motion for action." ~ Ernest Hemingway
- "If you hate a person, you hate something in him that is part of yourself. What isn't part of ourselves doesn't disturb us." ~ Herman Hesse
- "Whenever two people meet, there are really six people present. There is each man as he sees himself, each as the other sees him, and each as he really is." ~ William James
- Your time is limited, so don't waste it living someone else's life" ~ Steve Jobs
- "The true measure of a man is how he treats someone who can do him absolute no good." ~ Samuel Johnson

- "A champion is afraid of losing. Everyone else is afraid of winning" ~ Billie Jean King
- "Do not pray for an easy life, pray for the strength to endure a difficult one" ~ Bruce Lee
- "I don't know who my grandfather was. I am much more concerned to know what his grandson will be." ~ Abraham Lincoln
- "I am here for a purpose and that purpose is to grow into a mountain, not shrink to a grain of sand" ~ Og Mandino
- "You aren't born as yourself. You're born facing a mass of other people's ideas and preconceptions—and you have to mold a 'self' by working through those raw materials." ~ V.S. Naipual
- "The greatest thing a man can do in this world is to make the most possible out of the stuff that has been given me. This is success, and there is no other." ~ Orison Swett Marden
- "Life if you know how to use it, is long" ~ Seneca
- "Be hated. One does not have to be evil to be hated. In fact, it's often the case that one is hated precisely because one is trying to do right by one's own convictions. It is far too easy to be liked, one merely has to be accommodating and hold no strong convictions. Then one will gravitate towards the centre and settle into the average. That cannot be your role. There are a great many bad people in the world, and if you are not offending them, you must be bad yourself." ~ Adrian Tan
- "Being deeply loved by someone gives you strength, while loving someone deeply gives you courage." ~Lao Tzu
- "Care about what other people think and you will always be their prisoner." ~ Lao Tzu
- "The Journey of a thousand miles begins with a single step." ~ Lao Tzu
- "Those who know do not speak. Those who speak do not know." ~ Lao Tzu, Tao Teh Ching
- "Time is a created thing. To say 'I don't have time,' is like saying, 'I don't want to." ~Lao Tzu
- "Watch your thoughts, they become your words; watch your words, they become your actions; watch your actions, they become your habits; watch your habits, they become your character; watch your

character, it becomes your destiny." ~ Lao Tzu

- "Our greatest fear is that we are powerful beyond measure. It is our light, not our darkness, that most frightens us. Your playing small does not serve the world. There is nothing enlightened about shrinking so that other people won't feel insecure around you." - Marianne Williamson
- "If I try to be like him, who will be like me?" ~ Yiddish proverb
- "A human being is like a novel: until the last page you don't know how it will end. Or it wouldn't be worth reading." ~ Yevgeny Zamyatin
- "People often say that motivation doesn't last. Well, neither does bathing. That's why we recommend it daily." ~ Zig Ziglar

48. Renaissance (Man)

My life could be defined as an unquenchable hunger and thirst for knowledge. I studied Leonardo da Vinci when I was a little boy. Even at that age, I understood his gifts and that I wanted to be like him. I studied art and science for the rest of my life.

- Leonardo da Vinci
  - The Vitruvian Man is the best depiction of this well-rounded scholar.
    - It is the print I have above my bed as it speaks to who I am and what I wish to become.
    - I designed a book with my son being the 'Vitruvian Boy'. A future leader with a great base of knowledge to critically think and problem solve.
- Michelangelo
  - David (Michelangelo was only 26 when he was commissioned to create David)
    - 17 feet tall and 12,000-pound marble masterpiece.
    - It is one of the most important sculptures and stories for me. I went to the Galleria dell'Accademia in Florence, Italy to experience it. I only wish I had spent more time just enjoying the beauty of this work.

49. Sciences

Having a scientific mind or mindset is in my opinion one of the most important entrepreneurial skillsets you can have. There are a multitude of reasons for this comment being made and why I would devote a section to science in a dissertation on Entreprenology are for the following reasons:

- Data Analysis
  - Every business is rich in data and understanding how to read the data will allow the business to leverage and manipulate variables for optimum results.
    - Client data
      - Demographic data
    - Expense data
      - Marketing data
        - ROI data
    - Income data
      - Investment data
        - ROI data
      - Residual data
      - Sales data
- Problem Solving
  - If you can't solve problems, then you can't be an entrepreneur.
- Scientific Method
  - Necessary for even hypothesizing a result you wish to create.
- Trivia
  - The name of the radioactive element in smoke detectors in americium
  - J is the only letter that doesn't appear anywhere on the periodic table of elements.
  - There no mercury on Mercury … most of the planet is solid iron.

- o   Most-used metals in the world (in order): iron, aluminum, copper

Kenny loves black holes and often views youtube explanations of how different life would

Since I spent four years of my life teaching science and am currently teaching my 7-year-old son to appreciate and think like a scientist, I will share some of my favorite information here. Kenny has been the recipient of a deep dive into general science and advanced science knowledge. Sharing what I have been teaching him is causing me to rekindle my desire to teach children the application, discovery, importance and problems one can solve with an understanding of how to think like a scientist.

- • Anatomy – study of the parts of organisms
  - o During most of my seven years in college, this was a huge concentration of my reason for attending and studying... to become a medical illustrator. All I can say it ever did for me was make me feel a lot more confident in the doctor's office when explanations of my physical were discussed or presented.
- • Astronomy & Cosmology – study of the universe
  - o Kenny loves black holes and often views youtube explanations of how different life would be with a collision of a meteor or the sun getting a couple degrees hotter or closer, etc.
- • Biology – study of life
- • Botany – study of plants
  - o A focus I wish I had taken a lot more interest in when I was younger.
- • Dactylology – communication using fingers (sign language)
  - o My son and I communicate lightly with sign language. COVID gave us a lot more time to learn the importance of survival languages when you can't speak and only have your eyes and hands to communicate with.
- • Encephology – study of the brain
  - o Huge focus now on how the brain is healthier with the abundance and frequency of smiles.

- How the chemicals in our body shift because of the brain being in a state of bliss and joy.
- Entreprenology - study of cumulative wisdom, experience, and knowledge experientially & academically learned over the course of a professionals life as an entrepreneur.
  - Can you imagine how much better our planet would be if this course was offered from high school, through college?
  - You will see this focus is something I wish to integrate into schools and to make a mainstream word.
  - This study is in essence the study of how knowledge creates abundance.
- Gelotology – study of laughter
  - The ultimate study I will market to the world… even more than Entreprenology ☺
- Genetics – study of heredity
- Geology – study of rocks
- Hydrology – study of water
- Ichthyology – study of fish
- Meteorology – study of weather
- Philology – study of languages
  - I took a lot of Latin unsuccessfully to learn the root of language to explain science.
- Physics – study of energy & matter
  - The ultimate subject of science in my opinion. I devoted my education career to teaching this science.
- Psychology – study of human behavior
- Vexillology – study of flags
  - I have always loved studying this topic… What a fun course this would be to take in college.
- Zoology – study of animals
  - Groups of Animals – I have taught Kenny at least 40 names for groups of animals. I will share a couple here as they make me smile. Kenny is so proud he can name what agroup of almost any animal is called. We all know school of fish, pack of wolves, but these I learned during my dissertation. Why is this important?

I believe it is a further dive into how entrepreneurs could be grouped and why they should be grouped for their different behaviors, strengths and weaknesses. If you discover how to group entrepreneurs, you will probably unlock the magic collaboration or combination of ingredients ed to propel success. I great vision is nothing without a great play and a great system to implement the plan and cause an impact that results in a profit. Here are a few examples from Kenny's Fun Facts of Science:

- Group of camels is called a caravan
- Group of cats is called a clowder or glaring
- Group of elephants is called a parade
- Group of hyenas is called a cackle
- Group of lemurs is called a conspiracy
- Group of leopards is called a leap
- Group of lions is called a pride
- Group of owls is called a parliament
- Group of parrots is called a pandemonium
- Group of zebras is called a zeal

50. Successes

- Completion of Boy Scouts
- Completion of Landmark Curriculum for Living
  - The Forum
  - The Advanced Course
  - S.E.L.P.
  - I.L.P.

51. TED... Ideas worth spreading

- Malcolm Gladwell – Choices, happiness and spaghetti sauce
    - Howard Moskovitz, a psychophysicist about measuring things
    - The mind knows not what the tongue wants
    - Extra chunky tomato
    - To view - https://rb.gy/gajh0y
- Paul Piff – Does money make you mean?
    - Monopoly experiment
        - On the flip of a coin shows the demonstrative behavior of the 'rich' player vs. the 'poor' player.
        - Consume more pretzels
        - Louder
        - Believe they are intitled to their success and no correlation to the flip
    - Money mentality to Break the law more
    - Money mentality to Lie more
    - To view - https://rb.gy/qhticp
    - Brilliant look at how wealth mentality will do what it takes to have more even at the detriment of others (society)

52. Theories, Conspiracy and Otherwise... Shape Behavior

- Assassination of John F. Kennedy, Robert Kennedy, Malcolm X

53. TDIBH – This Day in Business History –
Historical Dates for Entrepeurology

- Jan. 1st, 1984 – AT&T is dismantled giving up its monopoly status.
- Jan. 10th, 1910 – Joyce C. Hall (a teenager boy) arrives in Kansas City, MO., and starts building a picture-postcard business into a giant of doggerel and cheer that would reshape American holiday celebrations. It commercialized holidays, which drove huge growth to the U.S. retailing with new bogus holidays invented.
  - Changed the abundance of my entertainment company.
  - We celebrated holidays and relationships with cards, and thematic music CD's
  - Wonderful way to show appreciation and is one of the most powerful ways to become a top of mind leader.
- Jan. 11th, 1964 – Surgeon General reports that smoking acuses lung cancer in men
  - In 1971, television and radio ads for cigarettes would be banned; in 1998, the industry would agree to pay $206 billion to settle state lawsuits over the public health costs of smoking, an unprecedented transfer of wealth from a legal private industry to the government.
- March 3, 1910
  - Rockefeller Foundation: John D. Rockefeller Jr. announces his retirement from managing his business so that he can be devoted full time to being a philanthropist.
- June 5th, 1947 – The Marshall Plan.
  - Two years after the end of World War II, Europe teeters on the

brink of chaos. While the U.S. booms, Europeans face rationing for basics like bread. In Britain, fishing fleets are kept in port for lack of fuel. In Germany, the economy seems to slide toward subsistence farming and the Middle Ages. Threats of starvation and Communism loom over Western Europe.

o So Secretary of State George C. Marshall gives a speech. But not just any speech. Marshall offers "substantial" U.S. assistance to help Europe rebuild after World War II. "The remedy lies in ... restoring the confidence of the European people in the economic future of their own countries and of Europe as a whole."

o With more than its usual foresight, Congress rapidly agrees, and from mid-1948 to 1951, the U.S. pours $13 billion worth of economic support and technical expertise into Europe. (That's almost $100 billion in 1999 dollars.) The aid gives Europe an immediate boost, spurring new investment and pulling the Continent out of its slump.

- June 18th, 1971 – Southwest Airlines begins flying.
  o Between Dallas, Houston and San Antonio.
- June 20th, 1975 – Steven Spielberg's movie 'Jaws' invariably opened gradually and tried to build an audience through word-of-mouth and limited advertising. Grosses $260M in the U.S. and introduces the concept of heavy preopening marketing and wide releases.
- June 21, 1834 - American inventor and business man Cyrus McCormick patents the reaping machine.
- June 22nd, 1944 – FDR signs GI Bill of Rights makes college and advanced training possible for millions of vets, dramatically increasing the education level and skills of the U.S. labor force
- June 29th, 1943 – Coca-Cola becomes a global brand during WWII.
- July 8, 2008 - American businessman T. Boone Pickens announces his 'PicKens Plan', an energy policy that moves away from imported oil.
- July 17th, 1955 – Disneyland opens in Anaheim, CA. The first major destination theme park spurs growth in travel and tourism nationwide. Walt Disney World in Orlando, FL., has more than 50,000 employees, is the largest single-site employer in the U.S.
- July 29th, 2958 – Eisenhower signs the act creating NASA

- Aug. 4th, 1930 – King Kullen store in Queens, NY, is the 1st to bring together the high volume and low cost that are hallmarks of the U.S. supermarket.
- Aug. 15th, 1914 – The French try to build a canal across the Panama isthmus connecting the Atlantic and Pacific oceans.
- Oct. 29th, 1996 – AOL goes to flat-rate pricing

"The world is a book and those who do not travel read only one page."
~ Augustine of Hippo

54. Travel...
'Don't tell me what you know... tell me where you've been'.

(Knocking out your bucket list)

Ken Rochon, Jr.

As an aside, I recognize all the flags of the countries I have visited, and my son has learned most of them as well.

I have published and written 3 children's books (Making Friends Around the World, Kenny's Favorite Things to Know, Be the Smartest Kid in the Room), a travel book (The Centurion World Traveller Game) and a coffee table photo book (Art of Travel).

At the age of 39, I realized I had not seen one country outside of North America since I was a child. I made a decision that I would purchase a digital camera and visit 100 countries before my 50th birthday. I talked to my good friend John Paul Berry, Jr. and asked him how this could best be done. He came up with a great plan of finding exotic trips that would help me add approximately 10 countries a year to my list. I was in agreement and at age 40, I when to Rome, Vatican City, and Greece to begin a long and expensive journey to fulfil one of my biggest bucket list items... 100 Countries documented with a digital camera and proof I had seen either the number one thing in that country or at least 3 of the top 10 things one should experience to count that country as visited.

I declared this journey by writing a book about the experience and how to get to 100 countries with this strategy. The 1st edition of 'The Centurion Traveler Game… Knocking Out Your Bucket List' was published around the point of me reaching the one third mark of my committed journey. I admitted that the book was not finished, although it reflected how to play the game and gave great information to that point on what to visit, what was dangerous, flag recognition, and other quotes and trivia.

The 2nd edition came out when I was at roughly 65 countries and again I admitted the journey was not complete, but it was on course to be complete if I continued with the strategies in the book. My final year was very strategic in that I ed to make sure that I hit the big 100 without disappointment. Ironically, the plan had me ending my 100th country in the MOST boring country on Earth… Lichtenstein. Wow, if Google asked why I would search this country to visit. My backup plan was that if any of the countries could not be visited because of weather, or poor planning, that I would have one more country to visit before I went home… Portugal. I landed in Lisbon, Portugal and was pleased at the dramatic difference the sites offered over Lichtenstein. So my 99th, 100th, and 101st countries had an 'L' component to being the 'L'ast. Luxembourg (Luxembourg City), Lichtenstein and Lisbon, Portugal.

The 3rd edition came out shortly after this accomplishment. It was the 2nd of 3 life long bucket list items… I only had one more thing to accomplish in life… be a father… and hopefully have a son I could pass my Father's name on to. Go to Father section of my dissertation to learn more about this experience.

Ultimate dream is to take my son with me around the world for about 100 days… to see the Wonders & the Challenges we face in the world. The poorest of conditions without coming back with malaria.

- Africa
  - Benin
    - Porto-Novo
  - Cape Verde
    - Praia
  - Egypt
    - Alexandria
    - Cairo
      - Pyramids of Giza
    - Port Said
  - Ghana
    - Accra
  - Madagascar - home to some of the world's most unique flora and fauna
    - Mozambique Channel
    - Lemurs
  - Morocco
    - Casablanca
    - Rabat
  - Namibia
    - Luderitz
    - Walvis Bay
  - South Africa
    - Cape Town
      - Kruger National Park
      - Table Mountain
  - Spanish Morocco
    - Ceuta
  - Togo
    - Lomé
- Americas
  - Central America
    - Costa Rica
      - Limon
      - San José
    - Panama
      - Colon
      - Panama City
  - North America
    - Canada
      - Ontario
        - Niagara Falls
      - Ottawa
      - Toronto
    - United States
    - Arizona
      - Phoenix
      - Tucson
    - California
      - Los Angeles
      - Sacramento
      - San Diego
      - San Francisco
        - Golden Gate Bridge
    - Colorado
      - Denver
    - Connecticut
    - Florida
      - Fort Lauderdale
      - Orlando
      - Tampa
    - Georgia
      - Atlanta
    - Hawaii
    - Illinois
      - Chicago
    - Indiana
      - Indianapolis
    - Louisiana
      - New Orleans
    - Maine
      - Portland
    - Maryland
      - Annapolis
        - Capital of

Maryland
- One of the Capitals of the United States
  - Ellicott City
    - Currently live here for twenty years
  - Fort Meade
    - Attended my Senior year of High School at Fort George G. Meade High School
- Baltimore
- Massachusetts
  - Boston
- Missouri
  - St. Louis
- Nevada
  - Las Vegas
    - Grand Canyon
- New York
  - Albany
  - Buffalo
  - New York City
    - Empire State Building
    - Statue of Liberty
- Ohio
  - Cleveland
- Pennsylvania
  - Philadelphia
  - Pittsburgh
- Rhode Island
  - Cranston
    - Dad's family lives here

- Providence
  - Dad went to college here
- Warwick
  - Born in Warwick
- Tennessee
  - Nashville
- Texas
  - Austin
  - Dallas
  - Houston
- Utah
  - Salt Lake City
- Vermont
- Virginia
  - Arlington
    - Arlington Cemetery
  - Richmond
- Washington
  - Spokane
- Washington, D.C.
- South America
- Argentina
  - Buenos Aires
- Brazil
- Rio de Janeiro
  - Christ the Redeemer
    - Located at the top of Corcovado mountain
    - Largest Art Deco statue in the world
    - 222 step climb from the train to the statue

- Chile
- Santiago
  - Attacked for 1st time
- Columbia
  o Bogotá
  - Honduras
  - Mexico
    - Accapulco
    - Cuernavaca
      - Studied Spanish for two summers. Each was a three-week immersion was hosted by a Spanish family each time. No English was permitted.
    - Mexico City
    - Puebla
    - San Juan
      - Teotihaucán Pyramids
  - Peru
    - Cusco
      - Machu Picchu
    - Lima
  - Uruguay
    - Montevideo
  - Venezuela
    - Caracas
- Asia
  o Cambodia
  - Siem Reap
    - Angkor Wat
      - It appears on the nation's flag
      - It is a 12th century 'temple mountain' built as a spiritual home for the Hindu god Vishnu
  o China
  - Beijing
    - Forbidden City
    - Great Wall of China
  - Dalian
  - Shanghai
  - Xi'an
    - Emperor Quinshihuang's Mausoleum Site Museum
      - The Terracotta Army is a collection of terracotta sculptures depicting the armies of Qin Shi Huang, the 1st Emperor of China. 210-209 BCE with the purpose of protecting the emperor in his afterlife.
  o Hong Kong
  o India
  - New Delhi
    - Lived there my 1st year of school

- Only white child in the school
- Uniforms
- Japan
  - Fukuoka
  - Hiroshima
  - Kyoto
  - Nagasaki
  - Tokyo (Largest city in the world)
  - Yokohama
- Malaysia
  - Kuala Lumpur
- Russia
  - Moscow
- Singapore
- South Korea
  - Busan
  - Seoul
- Taiwan
  - Taipei
- Thailand
  - Bangkok
- Ukraine
  - Odessa
  - Sevastopol (Now Russia)
  - Yalta (Now Russia)
- Vietnam
  - Hanoi
- Australia
- Australia
  - Sydney
- New Zealand
  - Wellington
- Caribbean
- Antigua & Barbuda
  - St. John's

- Aruba
  - Oranjestad
- Bahamas
  - Eleuretha
  - Nassau
- Barbados
  - Bridgetown
- Belize
- Bonaire
  - Krakeldijk
- Cayman Islands
  - George Town
- Curacao
- Dominica
  - Roseau
- Grenada
  - St. George's
- Jamaica
  - Kingston
  - Montego Bay
- Puerto Rico
  - San Juan
- Saint Kitts & Nevis
  - Basseterre
- Saint Lucia
  - Castries
- Saint Vincent & the Grenadines
- Sint Maarteen
- Trinidad and Tobago
  - Port of Spain
- Turks & Caicos Islands
- Europe
- Albania
  - Shkoder
- Austria
- Vienna

- Belgium
  - Antwerp
  - Bruges
  - Brussels
- Bosnia & Herzegovina
  - Sarajevo
- Bulgaria
  - Varna
- Croatia
  - Dubrovnik
  - Zagreb
- Czech Republic
  - Prague
- Denmark
  - Copenhagen
- Estonia
  - Tallinn
- Finland
  - Helsinki
- France
  - Cannes
  - Chambéry
    - Studied French three week immersion course
  - Lyon
  - Paris (Most visited city in the world)
    - Eiffel Tower
    - The Louvre (Largest museum in the world)
  - Rouen
- Germany
  - Berlin
  - Heidelberg
    - Attended 4th grade here
  - Karlsruhe
    - Attended 1st grade here
  - Stuttgart
    - Sister born there
    - Attended 2nd & 3rd grade
  - Warnemunde
  - Worms
    - Lived there 5th grade
- Greece
  - Athens
    - Acropolis
  - Mykonos
  - Santorini
- Hungary
  - Budapest
    - Buda's medieval Castle Hill
    - Neoclassical buildings along Pest's Andrássy Ave.
  - Danube River
- 19th-century Chain Bridge
- Iceland
  - Reykjavik
- Italy
  - Florence
    - Statue of David
  - Messina
  - Naples
  - Rome
- The Colosseum
  - Venice
- Gondolas
- Liechtenstein - One of the richest countries in the world per capita. My 100th country!

- Vaduz
  - Luxembourg
    - Luxembourg City
  - Montenegro
    - Podgorica
  - Netherlands
    - Amsterdam
      - Rijksmuseum, Van Gogh Museum
  - Norway
    - Oslo
  - Poland
    - Gdansk
  - Portugal
    - Lisbon
  - Romania
    - Bucharest
    - Constanza
  - Slovakia
    - Bratislava
  - Slovenia
    - Ljubljana
  - Spain
    - Barcelona
      - Antoni Gaudí's whimsical modernist landmarks
      - Sagrada Família Church
  - Sweden
    - Stockholm
    - Zurich
  - Switzerland
    - Bern
  - Turkey
    - Canakkale
    - Constantinople
    - Ephesus
- Istanbul
  - Hagia Sophia or the Blue Mosque
- Kusadasi
  - Vatican City - Smallest county in the world at 121 acres and a population of 825!
    - Roman Catholic Church
    - Laocoön and His Sons Sculpture
    - Sistine Chapel, famous for Michelangelo's ceiling
  - United Kingdom
    - England
      - Bath
      - London
      - Wiltshire
      - Stonehenge
  - Ireland
    - Dublin
  - Northern Ireland
    - Belfast
  - Scotland
    - Edinburgh
    - Glasgow
  - Wales
    - Cardiff
- Middle East
  - Bahrain
  - Israel
  - Bethlehem
  - Jerusalem
  - Jericho
  - Jordan
    - Amman
      - Petra is a famous

- archaeological site in Jordan's southwestern desert. Dating to around 300 B.C., it was the capital of the Nabatean Kingdom. Accessed via a narrow canyon called Al Siq, it contains tombs and temples carved into pink sandstone cliffs.
  - o Oman
    - ▪ Muscat
  - o Palestine
    - ▪ East Jerusalem
  - o Qatar - The richest country in the world!
    - ▪ Doha
  - o United Arab Emirates
    - ▪ Abu Dhabi
    - ▪ Dubai
  - o Burj Khalifa
    - ▪ Known as the Burj Dubai Skyscraper
    - ▪ Tallest in the world at 2,722 feet high
  - o Oceania of Atlantic
  - o Bermuda
    - ▪ Hamilton
  - o Oceania of South Pacific
  - o American Samoa
    - ▪ Pago Pago
  - o Fiji
    - ▪ Suva
  - o French Polynesia
    - ▪ Papeete
  - o Samoa
    - ▪ Apia

Travel Trivia
- The largest country in the world: Russia
- The border between Italy and Vatican City is marked by a painted white line.
- The smallest country in the world: Vatican City

Get your Centurion World Traveller shirt and start up conversations during your adventures in the world.

Price $29.95 plus S&H

info@theumbrellasyndicate.com or

202.701.0911 to order your shirt

55. Vegan Vitality

TOP 10 Vegan Vitality Epiphanies

1. Meat hardens blood vessels. A compound carnitine has been found to cause atherosclerosis, the hardening or clogging of the arteries.

2. Charring meat increases toxins (nitrosamines) that can lead to cancer of the stomach.

3. Meat contains 'lean finely textured beef (LFTB)," but the public knows it as 'Pink Slime'. This meat additive contains fatty bits of leftover meat that's heated, spun to remove the fat, and then treated with ammonia gas to kill bacteria.

4. Smaller cuts of meat are binded together into a larger serving can be done with 'meat glue' called transglutaminase, an enzyme formerly harvested from animal blood, but now produced through fermentation of bacteria.

5. Meat impacts the environment more than any other food we eat, mainly because livestock require much more land, food, water, and energy than plants to raise and transport. Producing a four-ounce (quarter pound) hamburger, for example, requires 7 pounds of grain and forage, 53 gallons of drinking water and irrigating feed crops, 75 square feet for grazing and growing feed crops, and 1,036 BTUs for feed production and transport—enough to power a microwave for 18 minutes.

6. "Your burger may contain meat from fewer than 10 cows or more than 1,000. The only way to know is ask the butcher—most states have laws

in place against fudging these facts that will not let them lie". The greater the number of cows in the hamburger, the greater the chance of contracting something that wasn't intended to be in the meat, he says. E. coli can cause dehydration, abdominal cramps, and kidney failure.

7. From locking animals in tiny cages, to slicing parts of their bodies off without any pain relief, to genetically selecting them to grow so obese and so fast that many become lame, it's by far the biggest cause of animal suffering in the world. Vegetarian protein sources provide nutrition without any such torture.

8. Diets rich in animal products contribute to the increased risk incidence of obesity as well as type 2 diabetes in the U.S. (e.g. a hot dog or 2 slices of bacon) daily led to a 19% and 51% increase in diabetes risk, respectively).

9. Meat contains a whole lot of iron which, when eaten in excess, can raise levels of iron in the brain and may increase the risk of developing Alzheimer's disease. When iron accumulates in the brain, myelin—a fatty tissue that coats nerve fibers—is destroyed. This disrupts brain communication, and signs of Alzheimer's appear.

10. Women who ate more than 1.5 servings (approximately 6 ounces) of red meat per day had nearly double the risk of developing hormone-sensitive breast cancer than women who ate 3 or fewer servings per week. Researchers believe the hormones or hormone-like compounds in red meat increase cancer risk by attaching to specific hormone receptors on the tumors.

SOURCE: https://www.prevention.com/food-nutrition/healthy-eating/
a20436097/10-reasons-to-stop-eating-red-meat/

A study found that 48% of soda fountains contain coliform bacteria, commonly found in feces.

56. Wisdom

- 'A person's success in life can be measured by the number of uncomfortable conversations he or she is willing to have' ~ Tim Ferris
- 'Income Circle Must Be Outside the Expense Circle to Experience Abundance' ~ Ken Rochon, Jr.
- Samuel Smiles – Author of 'Self-Help'

"Raise your words, not your voice. It is rain that grows flowers, not thunder."
~ Rumi

57. Words to Empower & Enrich Your Knowledge (Neology) ☺

These are words I focused on adding to my vocabulary during the dissertation and in some cases using to raise my sons ability to communicate confidently.

Ologie Power (Since this is a deeper dive, I will not repeat the more general studies of science that were covered in the Science section. This is the enlightenment of not just Entreprenology, but the awakening that there is are many disciplines to quench the thirst of anyone with a passion to solve a problem in this world... and beyond.

- Anemology – study of the wind
- Axiology – study of ethics, principles, & values
- Cetology – study of dolphins and whales
- Conchology – study of shells
- Dactylology – communication using fingers (sign language) Can't show that very well, but I love sign language!
- Dendrochronology – study of trees ages by counting their rings
- Deontology – study of moral responsibilities
- Encephology – study of the brain
- Entomology – study of insects
- Entreprenology - study of cumulative wisdom, experience, and knowledge experientially & academically learned over the course of a professional's life as an entrepreneur
- Eschatology – study of final events as spoKen in the Bible
- Gelotology – study of laughter

Taco Bell was sued for calling their taco filling "meat", because it contains more oats, seasoning and filler than meat.

- Hippology – study of horses
- Histology – study of tissues
- Hydrology – study of water
- Ichthyology – study of fish
- Meteorology – study of weather
- Morphology – study of the structure of organisms
- Mycology – study of fungi
- Myrmecology – study of ants
- Neology – study of new words
- Nosology – study the classification of diseases
- Oenology – study of wines
- Oology – study of eggs
- Osteology – study of bones
- Otology – study of ears
- Pathology – study of disease
- Phantomology – study of supernatural beings
- Philology – study of languages
- Pogonology – study of beards
- Potamology – study of rivers
- Psychology – study of human behavior
- Rhinology – study of noses
- Scatology – study of feces
- Semiology – study of signs and signaling
- Selenology – study of the moon
- Sinology – study of Chinese culture
- Toxicology – study of poisons
- Trichology – study of hair
- Vexillology – study of flags

Power Vocabulary I am learning or resurrecting in my communication. * = Misused

- Acuity - has to do with sharpness and smartness. Do you always get top grades in math? Then you have an acuity for numbers.
- Aficionado – a person who likes, knows about, and appreciates a usually fervently pursued interest or activity

- Ambidextrous – equally skillful with each hand
- Anagram – a word, phrase, or name formed by rearranging the letters of another, such as cinema, formed from iceman.
- Annihilated (v) - destroy utterly; obliterate
- Auspicious – indicating favorable circumstances and good luck
- Axiomatic (ak-see-uh-MAT-ik), adj. – taken for granted, self-evident
- Benefic (buh-NEF-ik), adj. – producing good or helpful results or effects.
- Bibliobibuli (n) - The sort of people who read too much. Etymology: The term was coined in 1957 by H.L. Mencken, who said "There are people who read too much: the bibliobibuli". From the Greek "biblio", meaning books, and the Latin "bibulous", from "bibere" (to drink).
- Dexterous (DEK-strus), adj. – mentally adroit and skillful, clever. Skillful and competent with the hands.
- Didactic – intended to teach, particularly in having moral instruction as an ulterior motive
- *Dilemma – specifically, a problem in which one must choose between two or more unsavory choices
- Doggerel is poetry that is irregular in rhythm and in rhyme, often deliberately for burlesque or comic effect
- *Enormity – evil
- Epithalamium – a poem written to celebrate a wedding
- Etymology - the study of the origin of words and the way in which their meanings have changed throughout history
- Forte – One's strong point
- Gamomaniac – an individual having an extreme enthusiasm or desire to be married, or in proposing marriage
- Garrulous – excessively talkative, especially on trivial matters
- Ineffable – incapable of being expressed or described in words: inexpressible
- Inquisitive – is a person that is inclined to investigate, eager for knowledge, unduly curious and inquiring
- Introspection - contemplation of your own thoughts and desires and conduct
- Juxtapose – to place side by side, especially for comparison or contrast
- Laconic - brief and to the point

- Lapidify - to turn into stone
- Lascivious – feeling or revealing an over and often offensive sexual desire
- Lethologica – is the inability to remember a word
- Lynchobite (n) - A person who works or labors at night and sleeps during the day.
- Melcryptovestimentaphiliac – a physiological compulsive disorder, in which a person has the sexual desire to steal lady's underwear for personal wear or sexual pleasure of smelling.
- Meliorism – the belief that the world tends to improve and that humans can aid its betterment
- Melliflous – flowing with honey, sweet sounding voices, syrupy tones, smoothly flowing speech or writing, it suggests a charming persuasiveness
- Metaphor - a figure of speech that suggests a non-literal similarity
- Multifarious – many and of various types
- Ne plus Ultra - the highest point capable of being attained
- Nebula - an immense cloud of gas and dust in interstellar space
- Nikhedonia The pleasure of anticipating victory or success. Etymologically from Nike, the Greek goddess of victory; plus hedone, pleasure.
- Olericulture – (n) – the cultivation of vegetables for the home or market
- Ombudsman - one that investigates, reports on, and helps settle complaints
- Omnivore - an animal that feeds on both animal and vegetable substances
- Onychophagia - is an oral compulsive habit of biting one's fingernails.
- Quidnunc – an inquisitive and gossipy person. Someone who asks too many questions
- Paradox – a statement or proposition that seems self-contradictory or absurd but in reality, expresses a possible truth.
- Pecuniary - consisting of or measured in money
- Perspicacious – having a ready insight into and understanding of things
- *Plethora – too much of something

- Promethean – (adj.) – creative; boldly original
- Propinquity – the state of being close to someone or something; proximity
- Quandary - state of uncertainty in a choice between unfavorable options
- Requite - to make return for: repay; to make retaliation for
- Stentorian (adj) sten-TOR-ee-un - extremely loud
- Superfluous – unnecessary, being beyond what is required or sufficient
- Tendentious – expressing or intending to promote a particular cause or point of view, especially a controversial one
- *Terrific = something that causes terror
- Travail (truh-VAIL), n. ` work especially of a painful or laborious nature; toil, labor, childbirth
- Tutelage (n) TOO-tuh-lij - instruction especially of an individual; a guiding influence; an act or process of serving as guardian or protector
- Ubiquitous - existing or being everywhere at the same time : constantly encountered
- Vacuous – having or showing a lack of thought or intelligence; mindless: 'a vacuous smile.'
- Verbiage - a profusion of words usually of little or obscure content
- Vicarious – felt or enjoyed through imagined participation in the experience of others
- Visage (VIZ-ij), n. – The face, countenance, or appearance of a person or sometimes an animal.
- Xenodochial - (adj.) a person, place or software application - that is friendly to strangers. "Xenos" is a Greek word for "strangers;", xenodochial means «hospitable.»
- Vocabulary Trivia
    - The only three English words that end in 'ceed': *succeed, proceed and exceed.*
    - The words 'flammable' and 'inflammable' mean the same thing
    - The longest one-syllable word in the English language: 'screeched'.

- The words 'loosen' and 'unloosen' mean the same thing
- Only word in the English language that begins and end with *'und'*: *underground*.
- The are only three words in English with the letters *'uu'* are vacuum, residuum, and continuum.

58. YouTube

This may be one of the most important parts of my dissertation because it carefully chooses videos that have expanded my heart and mind to be an entrepreneur and a leader who chooses to believe I can change the world. ☺

- America is Not the Greatest County in the World
  - https://www.youtube.com/watch?v=blpKfw17-yY
- Amplified Radio Show Interview Bert Oliva – 2016 76 views (17 min.)
  - https://www.youtube.com/watch?v=GBv_HCY7olk
- The Art of Code – Dylan Beattie
  - https://www.youtube.com/watch?v=6avJHaC3C2U
- Dr. Brené Brown on Empathy vs Sympathy
  - https://www.youtube.com/watch?v=KZBTYViDPIQ
- Chick-fil-A – Every Life Has a Story if You Bother to Read It (2010)
  - https://www.youtube.com/watch?v=2v0RhvZ3lvY
- Fatherhood: A Touching Story of an Old Father, son and a sparrow
  - https://www.youtube.com/watch?v=UVtm_fqGSng&t=248s
- The Greatest showman | "From Now On" with Hugh Jackman |20th Century FOX |(12.24.2017)
  - This is about resilience. Disasters become opportunities when hope is the lens you view life through.
  - This 1st link is even more meaningful because he had just been told he couldn't sing because of an operation to remove cancer from his nose.
  - https://www.youtube.com/watch?v=PluaPvhkIMU
  - This 2nd link is from the actual movie and my favorite part of the movie. It speaks to me probably more than any other song in a movie. Again, resilience and knowing you always have to the power to recreate yourself... it just takes getting back up and

believing. Thank you AAM.

- o https://www.youtube.com/watch?v=XyIDxpUJ10Q
- The Greatest showman | "This Is Me" with Keala Settle |20th Century FOX |(12.24.2017)
  - o This is the ultimate step into your power video I am so grateful to have witnessed. Thank you AAM.
  - o https://www.youtube.com/watch?v=XLFEvHWD_NE
- Ken Rochon
  - o Bert Oliva Mastermind Circle - 19 views (60 min.)
    - https://www.youtube.com/watch?v=v347wVHxq9o
  - o Calling Card (Perfect Networker) - 817 views (1 min.)
    - https://www.youtube.com/watch?v=v347wVHxq9o
  - o Ron Couming with Ken - 919 views (47 min.)
    - https://www.youtube.com/watch?v=ESecg4gRPSU
  - o ESTC 2018 – 1,727 views (37 min.)
    - https://www.youtube.com/watch?v=ESecg4gRPSU
  - o ESTC Science of Smiles 2019 - 598 views (47 min.)
    - https://www.youtube.com/watch?v=ESecg4gRPSU
  - o ESTC Sharing the Breakthrough Energy movement 2016 - 2,657 views (41 min.)
    - https://www.youtube.com/watch?v=ESecg4gRPSU
  - o Keep Smiling Movement
    - Carla Riechman GiggleFest Univsity 2020 18 views (52 min.)
      - https://www.youtube.com/watch?v=YvkZFenZzu8
    - Episode 3 – (Part 2) 2011 77 views (8 min.)
      - https://www.youtube.com/watch?v=UZJjmTUkzuQ
  - o Live Your Dream TV –
    - Episode 2 – 2011 242 views (8 min.)
      - https://www.youtube.com/watch?v=UZJjmTUkzuQ
    - Episode 3 – (Part 2) 2011 77 views (8 min.)
      - https://www.youtube.com/watch?v=UZJjmTUkzuQ
  - o The Mind Body Business Show – 9 view (60 min.)
    - https://www.youtube.com/watch?v=ZdXWGsLirwl
  - o MPI – Massive Positive Impact with James Allen – 1 view (30 min.)
    - https://www.youtube.com/watch?v=ESecg4gRPSU
  - o Muhammad Siddique 'Amplify Your Message on Facebook - 2014 (32 min.)

- https://www.youtube.com/watch?v=U2YQQq3gzuE&t=107s
○ NonProfit Performance with Hugh Ballou 'Engaging a Following' 33 views (35 min.)
  - https://www.youtube.com/watch?v=ESecg4gRPSU
○ Online Video Calling Card – 2009 360 views (1 min.)
  - https://www.youtube.com/watch?v=ESecg4gRPSU
○ PerfectNetworker (Photo Slide Show) 2009 – 1,514 views (3 min.)
  - https://www.youtube.com/watch?v=ESecg4gRPSU
○ The Service Hero Show with Tamara L. Hunter 2020 5 views (60 min.)
  - https://www.youtube.com/watch?v=A2XNeXMEVyc
○ The So Cal Business Poddcast Episode 2 1 view (60 min.)
  - https://www.youtube.com/watch?v=A2XNeXMEVyc
○ Speak in Dubai – 30 views (9 min.)
  - https://www.youtube.com/watch?v=A2XNeXMEVyc
○ Steve Taubman Testimonial – 19 views (1 min.)
  - https://www.youtube.com/watch?v=A2XNeXMEVyc
○ Tech With Heart "Tips To Scale Your Business or Social Movement (and K3) 2020 16 views
  - https://www.youtube.com/watch?v=Ok5Off6XTwE
○ The Umbrella Syndicate
  - CEO Space 1015 35 views
    - https://www.youtube.com/watch?v=gKe5aMJasZY
  - CEO Space Opening Ceremony 2015 24 views
    - https://www.youtube.com/watch?v=A-eKmo4XCdA
  - Centurion World Traveller presents Greg Horn Brazil World Cup 2014 31 views (1 min.)
    - https://www.youtube.com/watch?v=mf5Yc60nB7k
  - Federico Giller 2015 – 83 views (5 min.)
    - https://www.youtube.com/watch?v=mf5Yc60nB7k
  - Jon George "Interns are you Ready? 241 views (2 min.)
    - https://www.youtube.com/watch?v=kW0cHfj9wQo
  - Neva Lee Recia on CEO Space 2015 29 views (1 min.)
    - https://www.youtube.com/watch?v=_RcoipnO4qU
  - "The Power of One: Ken Rochon" 2013 - 2,243 views (3 min.)
    - https://www.youtube.com/watch?v=7IDcwQB0Fj4&t=24s
  - Secret Knock Superstar CEOs - 2015 - 552 views (2 min.)
    - https://www.youtube.com/watch?v=7IDcwQB0Fj4&t=24s

If humans consumed food like cows, they would have to eat 360 cheeseburgers and drink 400-800 glasses of water per day.

- Steven MacAlester "We do that... but.." 2013 - 174 views (1 min.)
  - https://www.youtube.com/watch?v=7lDcwQB0Fj4&t=24s
- TUS Children's Phonics Video Song Fortune 1000 – 2014 93 views (2 min.)
  - https://www.youtube.com/watch?v=7lDcwQB0Fj4&t=24s
- TUS Members ABC Children's Phonics Video Song –2014 235 views (2 min.)
  - https://www.youtube.com/watch?v=7lDcwQB0Fj4&t=24s
- TUS Tales From Around The World with Greg Horn – 2014 31 views (1 min.)
  - https://www.youtube.com/watch?v=7lDcwQB0Fj4&t=24s
- o Writer's Haven Show with V. Helena Rochon" 2019 - 59 views (29 min.)
  - https://www.youtube.com/watch?v=7lDcwQB0Fj4&t=24s
- Koolulam
  - o Believer | Imagine Dragons |Galgalatz | (10.10.2017)
    - Koolulam Project invited 600 people who had not known one another to the Bascula arts center in Tel Aviv, to sing together and kickstart the Galgalatz Radio annual international billboard.
    - https://www.youtube.com/watch?v=fQhj_aKQkBY
  - o Fix You | Coldplay |Across The Globe | (4.19.2020) (Online)
    - This pandemic has dictated a new reality, but we've taken this opportunity to overcome the obstacles and create together. Where there is creation - there is hope.
    - https://www.youtube.com/watch?v=h_7jvxBObaw
  - o I Lived by OneRepublic |South Africa | (10.14.2018)
    - Koolulam partnered with King David Schools, Johannesburg, South Africa, and gathered 3,500 South Africans to celebrate the 70th anniversary of King David Schools and the establishment of the State of Israel. Within 45 minutes, they learned a new arrangement of OneRepublic's "I Lived".
    - https://www.youtube.com/watch?v=vZrxTmNlYJs
  - o One Day by Matisyahu |Haifa | (2.14.2018)
    - https://www.youtube.com/watch?v=XqvKDCP5-xE
  - o One Love by Bob Marley |Tower of David | (6.14.2018)
    - In honor of the historic visit to Israel by Indonesia's religious leader Sheikh Haji Yahya Cholil Staquf, Koolulam invited 1,000 people who had never met before to a special event at the Tower of David in Jerusalem, to sing one song, in three languages and

in three-part vocal harmony. The event was produced in conjunction with the Tower of David Museum and Jerusalem.Com.
- Christians, Jews and Muslims who had never met before gathered at midnight, after the final day of Ramadan, to sing one song in three languages and in three-part vocal harmony.
- https://www.youtube.com/watch?v=TZzK29_V8jQ
  o Titanium - David Guetta Ft. Sia | Intl Women's Day| (2.26.2018)
    - Koolulam invited 2,000 women who hadn't met before to sing the song in a special empowering event organized by Na'amat marking International Women's Day.
    - https://www.youtube.com/watch?v=dk2kzQGvoYA
- Kris Krohn
  o https://www.youtube.com/watch?v=egW0JPUgVh0&t=371s
- The Mandelbrot Set
  o https://www.youtube.com/watch?v=56gzV0od6DU
- Simon Sinek
  o https://www.youtube.com/watch?v=IJyNoJCAuzA&t=773s
- Steve Jobs Insult Response (2016)
  o https://www.youtube.com/watch?v=0m9E9Ewhack&t=11s
- TED
  o Kyle McDonald
    - What if You Could a Paperclip for a House?
    - https://www.youtube.com/watch?v=8s3bdVxuFBs
  o Latif Nasser
    - The Amazing Story of the Man Who Gave us Modern Pain Relief (John J. Bonica)
    - https://www.youtube.com/watch?v=DokhOtMp75A
- Up In The Air
  o How Much Did They Pay You to Give up on Your Dreams?
    - https://www.youtube.com/watch?v=TkX-TPaodoM
- Veritasium – Dr. Derek Muller
  o 3 Perplexing Physics Problems
    - https://www.youtube.com/watch?v=K-Fc08X56R0
  o 13 Misconceptions About Global Warming
    - https://www.youtube.com/watch?v=OWXoRSlxylU
  o Why Are 96,000,000 Black Balls on This Reservoir? 59M views
    - https://www.youtube.com/watch?v=uxPdPpi5W4o

- o Be Hated (2014)
  - ▪ https://www.youtube.com/watch?v=0m9E9Ewhack&t=11s
- o Facebook Fraud
  - ▪ https://www.youtube.com/watch?v=oVfHeWTKjag
- o Is Success Luck or Hard Work? 2020 2M views
  - ▪ https://www.youtube.com/watch?v=3Lopl4YeC4I
- o Stringless Yo-Yo 2016 8M views
  - ▪ https://rb.gy/d8tuxw
- o Why Machines That Bend Are Better 2019 7M
  - ▪ https://rb.gy/vqi2jt
- o World's Roundest Object! (2013) 31M
  - ▪ https://rb.gy/cdcr73

59. Kenclusion

I have spent countless hours on this dissertation and am pleased after months of reviewing my experiences, my life and my new future how important this was to do now and not earlier. This accomplishment is my biggest and the one I am most proud of, because it is a cumulative look at learning, life and legacy. This opportunity is the first time I have thought about books I have read and yet forgotten what I learned. In revisiting all these experiences, I not only relearned what was forgotten, but I had new epiphanies that are fueling me to take on life at a whole new level.

60. Recommended Readings

- House of Leaves by Mark Danielewski
- The War of Art: Break Through the Blocks and Win Your Inner Creative Battles by Steven Pressfield

61. References

- Uncle John's Bathroom Reader
- Wikipedia
- Becoming the Perfect Networker by Ken J. Rochon, Jr., PhD
- Becoming Significant by David T. Fagan & Isabel Fagan
- Diagrams … An Explanation of Life by Ken J. Rochon, Jr., PhD
- Dream Life Planner by Noelle Peterson
- A Father-Son Bong by Ken J. Rochon, Jr., PhD
- Kenny's Favorite Triva Book by Kenny Rochon, III

62. Answers to Brain Teasers

- Answers to Numbers
  - If you took a single **penny** and **doubled** it **everyday**, by **day 30**, you would have $5,368,709.12
  - 1961 and 6009

- Answers to Brainteasers
  - 1. Throw it straight up in the air
  - 2. Push the cork through and then jostle the coin out of the bottle
  - 3. They are women
  - 4. The rope is not tied to anything else
  - 5. She is playing baseball or softball
  - 6. The police would have had to rewind the message to hear it
  - 7. He is playing Monopoly

- Answers to Riddles
  - 1. None. Moses did not have an Ark. Noah did.
  - 2. The Letter 'e'
  - 3. An equal
  - 4. Footsteps
  - 5. Gloves
  - 6. Heroine
  - 7. Memories
  - 8. Nothing
  - 9. Successfully, unsuccessfully
  - 10. Your word
  - 11. 'W'

Appendix

Awards & Certifications

- Art Summer Grant to Illinois State University (1981)
- Lifeguard Certificate (1982)
- Art Grant to Anne Arundel Community College (1982)
- Associates Degree Anne Arundel Community College (1985)
- Army Basic Camp Obstacle Record and Top 1% (1985)
- Bachelor of Science, University of Maryland, College Park (1987)
- Commissioned 2nd Lieutenant in United States Army (1987)
- Teaching Certification of Education for Science (1991)
- Governor's Academy of Science Teachers (1992)
- America's Most Influential Business Connector (2010)
- Entrepreneur of the Year (2018)

Birthday(s), Leo, and Year of the Dragon (1964)

One of the most powerful ways to show up in someone else's life is to send them a card and/or text celebrating their birth. I have a large database and card system for remembering important birthdays. I will not be including the names of them in this dissertation, however I will share what I am doing with birthdays to introduce my son to some of the people who have changed the world… and their birthday is a reminder that on that day we celebrate them coming into the world. I decided to also include what he is learning as some of the greatest leaders, problem solvers (scientists) are included in his birthday google searches.

- January 5th
  - o King C. Gillette, American Businessman & Inventor
    - As the 1st manufacturer of a razor with disposable blades, which would keep customers coming back.
- January 12th
  - o Jeffrey Preston Bezos Jorgensen (1964)
    - Founder of Amazon & Blue Origin
    - $204B
- February 8th
  - o Dr. Jim Omps
    - One of the most significant people for changing my life and acknowledging the importance of his work and how it impacts humanity
- February 15th
  - o Cyrus McCormick (1809), American Inventor and businessman (Mechanical Reaper)
- February 17th
  - o Thomas J. Watson, American Businessman. Chairman and CEO of IBM
- May 4th
  - o Andrea Adams-Miller, Executive Director of KSM
    - The reason it is a non-profit 501C
    - Access to so many influencers and leaders because of a strategic partnership that is priceless
- May 23rd
  - o Dr. Pauline Crawford-Omps
    - Married to the man who caused this dissertation and so much more to be created and inspired. ☺
- June 14th… Flag Day
  - o Kenneth James Rochon, III 'K3' is born ☺
- June 28th
  - o Elon Reeve Musk, Founder SpaceX, Tesla, Inc., PayPal, SolarCity
    - $98.5B
- July 17th
  - o Johann Jakob Astor (I) 1763
    - Known as the 1st Multi-millionaire business man in the United States
- July 18th
  - o Sir. Richard Charles Nicholas Branson, Author, Businessman, Investor and Former Philanthropist
    - Founded Virgin Group in the 1970s, which controls more than 400 companies in various fields.
    - $4.1B

- July 30th
  - Henry Ford (1863) died at 83
    - Founder of the Ford Motor Company
    - Pioneering a system that launched the mass production and sale of affordable automotives to the public
- August 1st
  - William Clark, American explorer who led the Lewis and Clark Expedition and claimed the Pacific Northwest for the United States, Ladysmith, VA
- August 2nd
  - Pierre Charles L'Enfant, French-born American architect who laid out Washington, D.C. Paris, France.
  - Frédéric=Auguste Bartholdi, French sculptor (designed the Statue of Liberty)
- August 5th
  - Neil Armstrong, astronaut, 1st man on the moon
  - David Corbin, Author, Speaker and brilliant problem solver and strategist
  - Reid Hoffman, American entrepreneur (co-founder of LinkedIn), born in Stanford, CA
  - Joseph Merrick, "The Elephant Man", born in Leicester, England (d. 1890)
  - Dr. Smiley... aka Ken J. Rochon, Jr., PhD ☺
- August 6th
  - 1928, Andy Warhol, one of the most influential artists of the latter part of the 20th century
- August 15th
  - Ben Affleck, American actor, film director, producer, 'Argo', 'Good Will Hunting'
- August 25th
  - Ken Rochon, Sr., My Dad, U.S. Army Officer, Retired
- August 31st
  - William Peach, Godfather to K3.
- September 1st
  - Johann Pachelbel, German composer (Canon in D)
    - I have played this beautiful classical piece at countless weddings... hundreds and hundreds. Given in my career I have done over 2,500 weddings, I should guess over half included ceremony and it was one of the most popular requests for the bridesmaids. So to say over 1,000 times this was played may not be an exaggeration.
- September 2nd
  - Keanu Reeves, Canadian actor and musician.
    - Reeves is perhaps best recognized for his role as Neo in The Matrix series (1999-2003)
- September 3rd
  - Shaun White, American Snowboarder
    - Courageous, overcame some serious spills
    - Has set records for gold medals and highest overall medal count
- September 4th
  - Beyoncé Giselle Knowles-Carter
    - Sold over 75 million records as a solo artist, and
    - A further 60 million with Destiny's Child
    - One of the best-selling music artists of all time
- September 5th
  - Freddie Mercury (full name Farrokh Bulsara), British singer-songwriter.
    - Front man for the British rock band Queen, and
    - One of their principal songwriters for such hits as "Bohemian Rhapsody" and "We are the Champions".

There are an average of 540 peanuts in a 12-ounce jar of peanut butter.

- September 6th
  - Dr. Janet Smith Warfield, founder of nonprofit Planetary Peace Power & Prosperity
    - Biggest needle move for the power of Keep Smiling books
    - Causing thought leaders to rally and be a part of her book
    - Big proponent of diagrams and science, planting the seed for me to do my "Diagrams... Explaining How Life Works" book.
    - Conscious Diagram (explained in attachment in "Diagrams"
    - $E=mc^2$ awakens my curiousity of Einstein and his brilliance.
  - Idris Elba, English Actor
    - Came to fame playing the character of Stringer Bell in HBO's critically acclaimed TV series "The Wire" (2002-08). Here in Baltimore, MD.
    - Ironically, Baltimore is the murder capital of the USA. Unfortunately, what Baltimore is known for is 'The Wire'.
    - Number 1 goal of Keep Smiling movement and this PhD is to wake Baltimore up that there are better choices... one is positivity, the other is choosing hope and leadership, and the right mentor(s).
- September 7th
  - Buddy Holly, American Singer songwriter.
    - Only 22 when he died in a plane crash
    - He remains one of the most influential rock and roll musicians.
- September 8th
  - Peter Sellers, 1925, probably the best depiction of perhaps who I wish to be. An actor, comedian, Favorite movie 'Being There' and Pink Panther series.
- September 9th
  - Adam Sandler, again a great entertainer and person I relate to. His movies in my opinion are brilliant and remind us as adults to still be a kid and have fun.
- September 10th
  - Colin Firth, English Actor. English film, television, and theatre actor
    - Films have earned more than $3 billion from 42 releases worldwide.
    - His most notable and acclaimed role to date has been his 2010 portrayal of King George VI in "The King's Speech", a performance that gained him an Oscar and many other worldwide best actor awards.
    - He has been a hero of mine as the characters he plays seem to embody who he truly is as a person.
- September 11th
  - Moby (Richard Hall), World deejay
- September 12th
  - H. L. MenchKen, known as the 'Sage of Baltimore', is regarded as one of the most influential American writers and prose stylists of the first half of the twentieth century
- September 13th
  - Gordon Thorn, Deejay and loyal friend of 37 years. One of the reasons my company AbsoluteEntertianment.com is still in operation and a possible legacy for my son. Should I wish to challenge him with a life of cyclic erratic entrepreneur life style.
  - Milton S. Hershey, Founder of The Hershey Chocolate Company, Born September 13, 1857, Derry Township, Pennsylvania, USA
- September 14th
  - Sam Neill, Irish (1947, 73 years old) actor, "Jurassic Park'
  - Tyler Perry, Actor, Director, & Producer
- September 15th
  - Marco Polo's pioneering journey to Central Asia and China inspired Christopher Columbus and many other travelers

- o Jen Rochon Herwig... my sister ☺
  - ▪ Mother of 2 wonderful children
  - ▪ Great family... American dream
  - ▪ Super successful HR career
- September 16th
  - o David Copperfield, American Magician
- September 17th
  - o Ken Kesey, US Author
- September 18th
  - o Aisha Tyler, Actress, comedian – I've met her, photographed her. Remarkable career.
- September 19th
  - o Jimmy Fallon, American actor and comedian and The Tonight Show.
- September 20th
  - o Sophia Loren, Italian actress
- September 21st
  - o Bill Murray, American actor and comedian
  - o Faith Hill, American country pop singer
- September 22nd
  - o Michael Faraday, English scientist discover electromagnetic induction, invented 1st electric motor.
  - o Andrea Bocelli, Italian tenor actress
- September 22nd
  - o Michael Faraday, English scientist discover electromagnetic induction, invented 1st electric motor.
  - o Andrea Bocelli, Italian tenor actress
- September 23rd WHAT A DAY!
  - o Augustus Caesar, 1st Roman Emperor (27 BC-14 AD),
  - o Kublai Khan, Mongol Emperor and founder of the Yuan dynasty in China,
  - o John Coltrane, American jazz saxophonist,
  - o Ray Charles, American singer and pianist who pioneered soul music,
  - o Bruce Springsteen (The Boss), American singer, songwriter and rock musician,
  - o Hasan Minhaj, American stand-up comedian (Patriot Act) – Favorite SHOW!
- September 24th
  - o Jim Henson, American puppeteer, artist, filmmaker (The Muppets)
- September 25th
  - o Christopher Reeve, American actor, Superman
  - o Will Smith, American actor and rapper actress
- September 26th
  - o Olivia Newton-John, Australian actress and singer
    - ▪ Grease changed my life... probably saw it over 30 times
- September 27th
  - o Gweneth Paltrow, American actress
- September 28th
  - o Confucius, Chinese philosopher
  - o Brigitte Bardot, French actress, model, animal activist
- September 29th
  - o Anita Ekberg, Swedish actress and Miss Sweden 1950
- October 1st
  - o William Boeing, American aviation pioneer who founded The Boeing Company
  - o Jimmy Carter, American, 39th US President, Plains Georgia
- October 2nd

Arachibutyrophobia is the fear of peanut butter getting stuck to the roof of your mouth and choking.

- o Mahatma Gandhi, 1869 Pacifist and Spiritual Leader, India.
- o Groucho Marx, 1890, Comedian, NYC.
- o Annie Leibovitz, American photographer (Rolling Stone), born in Waterbury, Connectcut.
- o Sting (Gordon Sumner), British singer-songwriter and bassist (The Police) and actor (Dune)
- October 3rd
  - o James Herriot (Alfred Wight), 1916, English veterinarian and novelist (All Creatures Great and Small).
  - o Chubby Checker, 1941, American singer-songwriter (The Twist, Limbo Rock), born in Spring Gully, South Carolina.
- October 4th
  - o Nelly Rochon, Mother to K3
- October 5th
  - o Denis Dederot, 1713, French enlightenment philosopher
  - o Robert H. Goddard, 1882, American Rocket Pioneer, (Invented and built 1st liquid-fueled rocket) born in Worchester, Mass.
  - o Ray Kroc, 1902, American fast food entrepreneur (McDonald's) and owner of San Diego Padres, born in Oak Park, IL.
  - o Bob Geldof, 1951, Irish singer (The Boomtown Rats) and activist (Live Aid).
- October 6th
  - o George Westinghouse, American entrepreneur and engineer (air brakes, alternating current system) born in NY
  - o Le Corbusier (Charles Jeanneret), Swiss French architect, city planner and artist (urbanisme).
- October 7th
  - o Niels Bohr, 1885, Danish physicist who expanded quantum physics (Nobel Prize 1922)
    - o Simon Cowell, 1959, English recording executive and television producer (X-Factor, American Idol, born London, UK.
- October 8th
  - o Matt Damon, 1970, American actor (Good Will Hunting, Ocean's trilogy, Bourne trilogy), born in Cambridge, Mass.
- October 9th
  - o John Lennon, 1940, English musician and member of The Beatles (Imagine), born in Liverpool, UK.
- October 10th
  - o Fridtjof Nansen, 1861, Norwegian Arctic explorer and advocate for refugees (Nobel Peace Prize 1922).
  - o Helen Hayes, American actress born in Washington, D.C.
  - o David Lee Roth, 1954, American rock singer (Van Halen), born in Bloomington, IN
- October 11th
  - o Amitabh Bachchan, Indian actor, film maker October 10th
- October 12th
  - o Hugh Jackman, Australian actor
- October 13th
  - o Sacha Baron Cohen, English actor and comedian
- October 14th
  - o Dwight D. Eisenhower, American President
- October 15th
  - o Mario Puzo, American novelist (The Godfather)

Career Experiences, Future Plans & Reflections

- Experiences
  - KAJARI Design (1982 – 1985)
  - KAJARI Sounds (1982 – 1988)
  - Laurel Art Center (1982-1988)
  - Construction Hand (Summer 1983)
    - Blue Collar experience 'College Boy'
    - Building Homes
    - Framing
    - Roofing
    - Transporting other workers
  - Hess Oil Company Gas Attendant (1983-1984)
    - Hustling & Scamming
      - Fake Oil changes
        - Down a quart with empty oil cans
    - Sting culture for who could hoodwink the most customers
      - Tips for service
  - Red Lobster (1 day)
    - Waiter – 1 day ☺
    - $25 tip for 1 table who felt sorry for me. ☺
    - Serving Food is demanding
  - Roy Rogers Restaurant (Summer 1983)
    - Expendable
    - Greasy, slippery and smelly
    - Roast Beef cutter and measuring portions
      - Measure less, eat more
    - Thankless
    - Unhealthy
  - Rochon, Brown & Associates Professional Disc Jockeys (1988-1995)
  - AbsoluteSounds Professional Disc Jockeys (1986-1991)
  - AbsoluteEntertainment.com (1991-2020 Current)
  - Prince George's County Public School System (1992 – 1996)
    - Nicholas Orem Middle School (Magnet School) (1992-1994)
      - Science Department Chair (1st year with 22 science teachers in my department
      - 8th Grade Physical Science School
    - Buck Lodge Middle School (Atlas School) (1994-1996)
    - 8th Grade Physical Science School

- o PerfectNetworker.com (2008-2012)
- o PerfectPublishing.com (2009-Current)
- o TheUmbrellaSyndicate.com (2013-Current)
- o TheKeepSmilingMovement.com (2015*-Current)
- o Live•Loco•Love Studios (2016-Current)
- o BIGeventsUSA.com (2018-Current) But not functional
- o Lyft (2019-Current)
  - Bought a VW Jetta 2014 to pay my car bills by ride sharing.
  - Learn the power of an app, automation, and programming to scale
- o Uber (2019-Current)
  - Used with Lyft to help pay car bills and have a back up car in case my cars were rented on Turo
  - Learned how the app gamifies earning ratings, and high stats. Much more advanced then Lyft with this gamification.
- o Turo(2019-Current)
  - Purchased a Smart car to ensure I had a back up charge while my Tesla was charging for client rentals.
  - Help supplement my car payments by renting my Smart car and Tesla
- o BeeKonnected.com (2020-Current)

'Resist the temptation to get a job. Instead, play. Find something you enjoy doing. Do it. Over and over again. You will become good at it for two reasons: you like it, and you do it often. Soon, that will have value in itself.' ~ Adrian Tan

- Career Future Plans Experiences
  - o 1 Year
    - Children's Book series in schools
    - Curriculum written for children's book series
    - Doctorate completed
    - 1000 Keep Smiling Book System
    - Perfect Publishing has 21 children's books it is marketing to schools
  - o 3 Year
    - 50 languages that Keep Smiling books and cards represent
    - 10,000 Keep Smiling Books
  - o 5 Year
    - 50,000 Keep Smiling Books

- o 10 Year
  - 100,000 Keep Smiling Books
  - Financially Independent with house paid off
- o Legacy
- Career Reflections
  - o Least Useful Academic
    - Almost all of my time at University of Maryland at the College Park Campus
    - Classes were huge, instruction was boring, no interaction with instructors.
    - Malcolm Gladwell's 'David and Goliath shares the experiment of how we rarely stop to consider whether the most prestigious of institutions is always in our best interest.
    - The Big Pond Institutions enroll really bright students and demoralizes them.
    - Had a gone to smaller classes, institutions, I would have enjoyed the experience, attended classes and earned a much better education.
    - This was an example of NOT quitting, was a bad idea. Hindsight right?
  - o Most Useful Academic
    - Howard Community College is the best all-around experience for being engaged, and having interactive opportunities with the instructor.
      - All the languages were taught by caring instructors who wanted you to be successful.
      - Although the teaching of the languages ended up being completely unhelpful for feeling confident or applying the language in real life, it was good for general pronunciation and culture.
  - o Least Useful Non-Academic
  - o Most Useful Non-Academic
  - o Advice
    - Accounting System
    - Agreements of Understanding … Signed
    - Vet Everyone
  - o Breakthroughs
    - Sales
      - Alternative Closing

In the USA, a pound of potato chips costs two hundred times more than a pound of potatoes.

- Giving 2 choices increased psychological commitment to going with the sales person
- Breaking limiting mindsets
  - We believed a sales person could only close $9,000 in a month
  - When we shattered this belief, we soared to $20K a month, then $40K and as a company over $100K a month.
- Packages
  - Discounting through combining services to increase weaker services being included and closed for higher profit.
- Upselling
  - Creating an A la Carte menu to increase invoice and profits
    - Lighting packages increased sales an average of $300
    - Extra speakers increased sales on average $200
    - Selfie Machine increased sales on average $400
- Value adjustments
  - Over time I have evaluated my time to be worth $10 an hour and that jumped when I became a deejay to $100 an hour. I started doing weddings at $500 for an entire event. When I moved my price to $800 it almost shocked the industry whose average was closer to $400 to $500. A photographer told me to move my price over $1000 and I was extremely scared to go to four figures. For about three months I was hesitant because I would be saying I was twice as expensive as the best deejay in Washington D.C. I launched my new price, and sold even more. I adjusted my rate roughly $500 a year and it matured around $2500 which was still about $1000 more than any other company. We closed at over 80% of our events. This kept over forty deejays actively busy performing over 1,400 events that particular year.
- Creative & Innovative Highlights
- Crisis
- Events that prepared and/or shaped
  - Paper route

- Collections
- Deadbeats
- Huge lesson in accountability
- Sales and enrolling people to buy
- Work Ethic
    - Failures Points
        - Accounting without accountability
            - Embezzlement (over $150K)
        - Conflicts of Interest
        - Hiring without vetting
        - IT overcharging, and sabotage
    - Mindset
        - Abundance vs. Scarcity
        - Assumptive Close & Relationship
    - Philosophies
        - Rule of 3
            - Happy to Buy/Hire for
            - Happy to Own for
            - Happy to Work for
    - Success Strategies
        - Hire Character
        - Integrity = Work Ethic
    - Turning Points
    - Least Successful Period
    - Most Successful Period
    - USPs (Unique Selling Position)

Colleges

- Anne Arundel Community College, MD   (AACC)   1982-1985
- Catonsville Community College, MD   (CCBC)   1996
- Howard Community College, MD   (HCC)   1991-2010
- Illinois State University, IL   (ISU)   1981
- Johns Hopkins University, MD   (JHU)   1985-1987
- University of Maryland, College Park, MD   (UMCP)   1985-1987
- University of Maryland, Baltimore Campus, MD   (UMBC)

College Courses (N=Audit / NO GRADE)

AMSL-101	Elementary Sign Language	(HCC)	C	1.2007
AMST298A	Popular Music 1945-Pre	(UMCP)	B	1.1986
ARAB 101	Elements of Arabic I	(HCC)	A	9.2004
ARC 111	Architectural Drawing I	(AACC)	B	1.1983
ARC 121	Architectural Materials & Methods I	(AACC)	B	1.1983
ART 102	Three Dimensional Design	(AACC)	A	9.1983
ART 125	Basic Drawing I	(AACC)	A	9.1982
ART 126	Basic Drawing 2	(AACC)	B	1.1983
ART 130	Printmaking I	(AACC)	A	1.1984
ART 131	Painting I	(AACC)	B	1.1983
ART-148	Digital Imaging, Raster Prog. I	(HCC)	N	9.2010
ART 210	History of Western Art II	(AACC)	C	1.1984
ART-280	Web Design & Production I	(HCC)	N	9.2010
ARTS340	Elements of Intaglio	(UMCP)	A	1.1988
ART 392B	Creative Thinking Humans	(UMBC)	A	7.1988
ARTS418B	Drawing	(UMCP)	A	1.1988
ARTT-112	Introduction to Digital Media	(HCC)	N	1.2011
ARTT-130	Introduction to Video I	(HCC)	N	1.2011
BIO 103	Fundamentals of Biology	(AACC)	A	9.1982
BIO 105	General Zoology	(AACC)	B	1.1983
BIO 231	Human Biology I	(AACC)	N	9.1984
BIO 233	Anatomy & Physiology I	(AACC)	C	1.1985
BIOL103	Biology Topics in Mod Soc	(UMBC)	A	7.1991
BPA 111	Intro to Business	(AACC)	B	9.1983
BPA 142	Principles of Management	(AACC)	C	9.1983
BPA 211	Principles of Accounting I	(AACC)	C	1.1984
BU-100	Intro to Business & Org	(HCC)	A	1.1997
BY-200	Microbiology	(HCC)	A	1.1991
BY-201	Genetics	(HCC)	B	1.1991
CH-201	Organic Chemistry	(HCC)	B	7.1992
CHE 111	General Chemistry I	(AACC)	B	1.1985
CHNS-101	Elementary Mandarin Chinese	(HCC)	N	9.2006

•	CM-106	Successful Learning Strategies	(HCC)	A	1.1991
•	EC-101	Principles of Economics Macro	(HCC)	A	9.1996
•	EDHD350	Factors Personal Development	(UMCP)	B	9.1988
•	EDHD411	Childl Growth & Development	(UMCP)	C	8.1988
•	EDHD413	Adolescent Development	(UMCP)	B	8.1988
•	EDP 113	Data Processing	(AACC)	B	1.1984
•	EDP 138	Programming in Basic	(AACC)	B	9.1984
•	EDPA301	Foundations of Education	(UMCP)	B	1.1987
•	EDHD306	Study of Human Behavior	(UMCP)	A	1.1988
•	EDUC300	Principles Secondary Education	(UMBC)	A	9.1991
•	EDUC308	Field Exp: Secondary Education	(UMBC)	A	9.1991
•	EDUC332	Science: Secondary School	(UMBC)	C	1.1992
•	EDUC340	Educational Psychology	(UMBC)	A	9.1991
•	EDUC401	Student Teaching Secondary	(UMBC)	A	*
			(10 CRED)		1.1992
•	EDUC408	Sr Seminar Secondary Education	(UMBC)	A	1.1992
•	EDUC487	Mainstreaming	(UMBC)	B	9.1991
•	EG-180	Vocabulary Development	(HCC)	A	1.1997
•	ENG 111	Comp & Intro Lit I	(AACC)	B	9.1982
•	ENG 112	Comp & Intro Lit 2	(AACC)	B	1.1983
•	ENGL393	Technical Writing	(UMCP)	A	1.1987
•	FREN-101	Elements of French I	(HCC)	B	1.2004
•	FREN-102	Elements of French I	(HCC)	B	1.2006
•	FREN-102L	Elements of French I Lab	(HCC)		1.2004
•	FREN-201	Intermediate French I	(HCC)	C	9.2004
•	FREN-202	Intermediate French II	(HCC)	A	1.2004
•	FREN-202L	Intermediate French II Lab	(HCC)		1.2004
•	GREK-101	Intro to Modern Greek	(HCC)	A	9.2006
•	GREK-102	Elementary Modern Greek II	(HCC)	N	1.2007
•	HIS 111	History of Western Civ I	(AACC)	B	9.1982
•	HIS 212	History of US 2	(AACC)	B	7.1985
•	HNDI-101	Elementary Hindi I	(HCC)	A	9.2010
•	ITAL-101	Elementary Italian I	(HCC)	B	9.2004
•	ITAL-101L	Elementary Italian I Lab	(HCC)		9.2004
•	ITAL-102	Elementary Italian II	(HCC)	B	9.2004
•	ITAL-102L	Elementary Italian II Lab	(HCC)		9.2004
•	LFIT-126	Yoga I	(HCC)	N	9.2010
•	LFIT-920	Body Sculpting	(HCC)	N	9.2010
•	NUTR-211	Nutrition	(HCC)	N	9.2010
•	PSY 111	Intro to Psychology	(AACC)	C	1.1984
•	PSYC235	Psychology of Adjustment	(UMCP)	C	9.1988
•	PSYC285	Abnormal Psychology	(UMBC)	A	7.1988
•	PSCY332	Psychology of Human Sex	(UMCP)	C	9.1988
•	MAR 101	Marketing Management	(CCBC)	A	1.1996

Strawberry contains about 200 seeds on its surface and is the only fruit with seeds on the outside of the fruit. 181

•	MATH111	Intro to Math II	(UMCP)	B	9.1987
•	MAT 112	Business Mathematics	(AACC)	B	9.1984
•	MAT 191	Calc & Analytic Geom I	(AACC)	C	7.1985
•	PE-129	Self Defense	(HCC)	A	1.1996
•	PHE 102	Weight Training	(AACC)	A	9.1982
•	PHE 127	Indoor (Box) Soccer	(AACC)	A	1.1984
•	PHE 145	Tennis I	(AACC)	B	9.1982
•	PHE 149	Soccer	(AACC)	A	1.1984
•	PHE 233	Weight Training	(AACC)	A	1.1983
•	PHE 250	Intro to Lifetime Sports	(AACC)	A	1.1984
•	PHE 256	Swimming I	(AACC)	B	1.1983
•	PHE 281	Skills Lab Softball	(AACC)	B	1.1984
•	PHE 289	Skills Lab Racquetball	(AACC)	B	1.1984
•	PHED1460	Racquetball Int	(UMCP)	A	1.1987
•	PHED340	Coaching Athletics	(UMCP)	B	9.1987
•	PL-202	Logic & Critical Thinking	(HCC)	A	9.1996
•	PS-103	General Physics	(HCC)	A	7.1991
•	PSY 111	Intro Philosophy (UMCP)	PASS		9.1988
•	RDG 011	Read & Study Skills (AACC)	PASS		7.1982
•	RTVF314	Intro to Film	(UMCP)	C	9.1986
•	RUSS-101	Fdnl Russian I	(HCC)	A	1.2006
•	RUSS-202	Int Russian II	(HCC)	N	9.2007
•	SABR-901	Mexico – Language Study Abroad	(HCC)	A	12.2007
•	SC-104	Elementary Astronomy	(HCC)	A	1.1991
•	SOCY325	Sex Roles	(UMCP)	C	1.1987
•	SPAN-101	Elementary Spanish I	(HCC)	B	9.2004
•	SPAN-102	Fdnl Spanish II	(HCC)	A	1.2006
•	SPC 111	Fundamentals of Oral Comm	(AACC)	C	7.1983
•	TURK-101	Fdnl Turkish I	(HCC)	N	9.2011

"If we could change ourselves, the tendencies in the world would also change. As a man changes his own nature, so does the attitude of the world change towards him. We need not wait to see what others do."

~ Mahatma Ghandi

WHY WORRY DIAGRAM

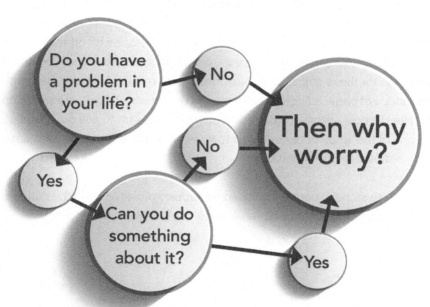

TheKeepSmilingMovement.com

FREE Strips of Paper!!!

PerfectWorldNetwork.com understands there are times when you don't have a place to take notes so we are providing these convenient strips of paper at the bottom of this sheet so you can write down some of the ideas you have after reading this book. Feel free to use the strips of paper to make mini airplanes, or to wrap up your bubble gum. Share these strips with others and see how much fun you can have in a group .We would like to hear from you about other uses for these strips, as we are considering make a full color book with these strips of paper (of course still available only in white). If you are someone who likes to cook or travel extensively then you will want to see our new skit. Use one of the strips of paper below to write this email address to get a copy of the skit (Ken@KenRochon.com).

Again, these strips of paper have been generously provided by all the partners of the Perfect Office in conjunction with the PerfectWoldNetwork.com

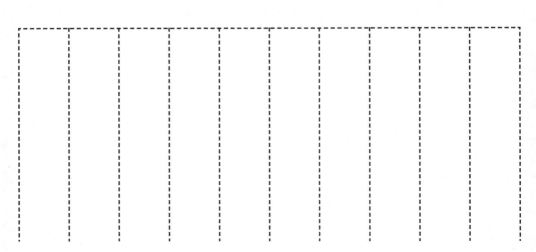

About the Author

This is a short 'Bio' used for introductions to podcasts, radio and speeches.

Born in Warwick, Rhode Island to a military family life, he has seen the world and currently resides in the Washington, D.C. metropolitan area.

Ken is a renaissance man, humanitarian, and an accomplished serial entrepreneur, established his successes with The Umbrella Syndicate, Perfect Publishing, & Absolute Entertainment. He is a Social Proof Celebrity Event Photographer, International Keynote Speaker, and Published Author of 30+ books. He is the Co-Founder of the non-profit organization "The Keep Smiling Movement," a radio host on Voice America Influencer Channel, and has been honored as "America's Most Influential Business Connector" and "Entrepreneur of the Year."

Ken's focus is supporting and promoting great leaders, authors, and speakers. He helps businesses grow using "Amplification" strategies in their event and product campaigns. His company gets over 100,000 clicks and engagements a week, making it one of the most active social media pages. He has exceeded one thousand (1000) 5-star reviews making him one of the most recommended businesses worldwide.

Ken, who lost his mother to Alzheimer's, desires to live a life of purpose where he leaves a legacy of love for his son to model.

He loves the arts and sciences, and he has traveled to over 100 countries. His favorite place to be is with his son Kenny aka 'K3', the light of his life.

More Books From

PERFECT PUBLISHING

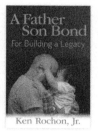

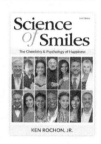

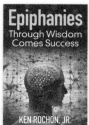

www.PerfectPublishing.com